FAMOUS DEAD CANADIANS 2

by
Joanne Stanbridge

Illustrated by
Bill Dickson

Scholastic Canada Ltd.
Toronto New York London Auckland Sydney
Mexico City New Delhi Hong Kong Buenos Aires

Scholastic Canada Ltd.
604 King Street West, Toronto, Ontario M5V 1E1, Canada
Scholastic Inc.
557 Broadway, New York, NY 10012, USA
Scholastic Australia Pty Limited
PO Box 579, Gosford, NSW 2250, Australia
Scholastic New Zealand Limited
Private Bag 94407, Greenmount, Auckland, New Zealand
Scholastic Children's Books
Euston House, 24 Eversholt Street, London NW1 1DB, UK

Library and Archives Canada Cataloguing in Publication
Stanbridge, Joanne, 1960-

Famous dead Canadians 2 / Joanne Stanbridge ; illustrated by Bill
Dickson.

ISBN 0-439-95729-X
1. Canada—Biography—Humor—Juvenile literature. I. Dickson, Bill
II.Title.

FC25.S732 2006   j920.071   C2006-900955-4

6 5 4 3 2 1   Printed in Canada   06 07 08 09 10

To my friends and colleagues at
KFPL, for patience and good humour
in the face of all my "Deads."

Acknowledgements:

Special thanks go to the whole amazing team at Scholastic Canada, Lori Burwash for her painstaking fact-checking, Wilson Kerr of Chatham and Lee Dickson of Toronto for photos and research assistance, my writing friends for much encouragement and valuable feedback, and my family — as always — for cheerleading and moral support above the call of duty. Many thanks!

TABLE OF CONTENTS

iNTRODUCTiON: SOMETHiNG AWFUL

Something terrible has happened. It hurts me to tell you about it. Would you pass me a rag? I want to wipe my hands. It's very greasy down here under my big black taxi.

Pardon? No, the taxi isn't broken. This problem is even worse. My secret project is missing! I thought it might have fallen into the engine, but I've poked through all these wires and pipes, and it just isn't here. It was the most important project I've ever done. And now it's gone.

It was safely locked up in my brown briefcase with the broken handle. I'm sure I carried it on my most recent *Plumley Norris Field Trip and Historical Excursion™*. I was helping another group of students with their assignments, but I'm afraid they were not as helpful or polite as you are. I was very busy trying to keep them from falling into rivers and getting into trouble with the police. In the confusion, maybe I left my briefcase under a tree. Or in a helicopter. Or in a graveyard. Oh, dear.

I've searched everywhere for it. It contains my secret project. It's something amazing. Something that will revolutionize the way young people learn about Canadian history. Something that will astonish my former colleagues at the Extremely Important Institute of Canadian Studies (EIICS) and make them *beg* me to come back.

What is it? Sorry, I can't possibly tell you. It's top secret. But I *must* find that briefcase. My whole future depends on it.

Pardon? Did you say you would help me look for it? Goodness! Young people these days are extremely kind. Are you sure you have time? Are you sure you don't have homework assignments to complete?

Ah. You *do*. Your teacher wants you to write about the lives of some famous dead Canadians.

Well, perhaps we can help each other. While we retrace the stops I made during my previous excursion, you can help solve my briefcase mystery. (You don't mind starting at the *end* instead of the *beginning*, do you? No? Excellent!) Your young eyes might spot some clues that I overlooked. And I can help you with your research. I'll tell you about some famous and not-so-famous dead Canadians. Our journey will be quick and fun and mysterious. Your assignments will soon be written, and maybe — just maybe — we'll find that briefcase.

I feel better already.

There's no time to lose. Jump into the big black taxi. Give me your permission slips and fasten your seatbelts. Adjust your deerstalker hats, polish your magnifying glasses and open your notebooks.

Welcome to the *Plumley Norris Field Trip and Historical Excursion (Mysterious Edition)*™.

Plumley Q. Norris

TOMMY DOUGLAS: THE GREATEST CANADIAN

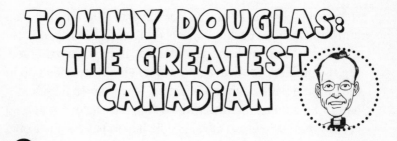

Oh, I *hope* we'll find my lost briefcase! Let's retrace the steps of my last *Historical Excursion™*, which ended here in Regina, Saskatchewan. I'll park the big black taxi in front of the T.C. Douglas Building, and while we search for the Lost and Found, I'll tell you about **THE GREATEST CANADIAN.** You're sure to write an essay that will make your teacher shout with joy.

If you ask ten people who this building is named for, nine of them will probably say "Tommy!!" (The tenth will probably say "I dunno," but there are always people like that, aren't there?) Some of the people will remind you that Tommy Douglas was voted **THE GREATEST CANADIAN** in a huge contest in 2004. I'll tell you why.

He was born in Scotland in 1904. When he was six years old, his family moved to Winnipeg. (That's why he's called **THE GREATEST CANADIAN**. Otherwise we'd have to call him the **GREAT SCOT**, which is not the same thing at all.)

A person doesn't get to be **THE GREATEST CANADIAN** by giving up when things get tough. All his life, Tommy was a fighter and a survivor. When he was a boy, times were bad. There wasn't much money. One day he fell down and cut his knee badly on a rock. For four whole years he was in constant pain. He was in and out of hospital. But did that stop him from going to school and playing with his friends? No way! Even after the bone got infected, Tommy stayed brave. But the problem got worse and worse. Finally he ended up in the hospital with a serious infection. It was spreading, and it had to be stopped before it killed him. He needed a special operation. But in those days, people had to pay for their own medical care, and Tommy's family was poor. They couldn't afford to pay for a specialist to do the operation. There was only one thing to do. The doctors decided to cut off Tommy's leg.

Oh, I'm sorry! Oh, dear . . . I shouldn't have sprung it on you like that. Please sit down until the room stops spinning. Are you all right?

Don't worry. When **THE GREATEST CANADIAN** grew up, he still had both legs. A specialist just happened to be visiting the hospital where Tommy was staying. The doctor offered to operate on his leg for free, as long as some medical students could watch the operation. And guess what? YES! Tommy got better.

For the rest of his life, Tommy was grateful for that doctor's help. But one thing bothered him. It didn't seem fair that his leg (and his life) had been in danger just because his family was poor.

Why couldn't medical care like that be available to *everyone*, rich or poor?

Oooh! How clever you are! Yes, you're right — **THE GREATEST CANADIAN** vowed to change the system. Later he said, "Through the years I came to believe that health services ought not to have a pricetag on them." To a young Canadian like yourself, that might sound like plain common sense. But in those days, there was nothing common about it. **THE GREATEST CANADIAN** would shock a lot of people with his big idea. But first he had some growing up to do.

Tommy's family was so poor that he and his sisters sometimes had to drop out of school for a while to help pay the family's bills. When he was just fourteen, Tommy left school for good and went to work in a printing shop.

One Saturday, while Tommy and his friend Mark were wandering around downtown Winnipeg, they saw something they would never forget. The parks and streets were filled with workers who had gone on strike. Tommy and Mark heard a commotion, but instead of going straight home like sensible young people, they climbed onto the roof of a building to get a better view. From there they saw a terrifying scene. Mounted police rode straight into the crowd, first one way and then another, breaking up the strikers' parade. Several hundred civilian "deputies" with sticks and baseball bats joined the police, beating the protesters and trying to scare them away. On a nearby street, the police opened fire on the crowd and killed a man.

Later the army arrived with machine guns to patrol the city. Those terrifying days would go down in Canadian history. The Winnipeg General Strike lasted for five more days, and Tommy never forgot what he had seen on "Bloody Saturday."

THE GREATEST CANADIAN was small but he was feisty. In his spare time, he took up boxing, and within three years he became the amateur lightweight boxing champion of Manitoba. Then he decided to go to college. For a guy who had dropped out of school, college was a struggle. But Tommy was an expert at hard work. With the same grit that had helped him survive in the hospital and the boxing ring, he threw himself into his studies. When he was done, **THE GREATEST CANADIAN** had two university degrees, a wife and a new job as a church minister in Weyburn, Saskatchewan.

All around him, people were suffering. The Great Depression had left many without jobs or money. A drought killed all the crops and turned the fields to dust. Then a plague of grasshoppers ate everything in sight. The crops were completely gone. The farmers had no money. Once again Tommy got to see what happened when people couldn't afford to pay for doctors. Sometimes he had to beg or borrow money while a patient sat in the doctor's waiting room. Sometimes the patient would die and Tommy would have to conduct the funeral service.

At that time, a new political party was taking hold in Saskatchewan, and Tommy liked what it was saying. The party was called the Co-operative Commonwealth Federation, or CCF. Its members believed that the government should get involved with banking, hospitals, workers' wages and farming. This sounded dangerous to people who believed in the old system, where the government pretty much stayed out of these things. But to Tommy the CCF sounded like a step in the right direction. So in 1934 he tried to get elected to the Saskatchewan government. He didn't win, and his bosses in the church told him to stop getting involved in politics. If he didn't, he could lose his job as a minister. But Tommy ignored them. The next year there was a federal election, and he ran again. This time he won. He was on his way to Ottawa, to represent his community in the government of Canada.

Tommy was young and inexperienced, but that didn't make him shy. In his first session of Parliament, he gave sixteen speeches. The prime minister was so impressed that he offered Tommy a place in his own political party. But Tommy said no because he was committed to the CCF's beliefs.

Tommy served in the federal government for nine years. Then he became the leader of the Saskatchewan CCF Party and ran for a new job: premier of Saskatchewan.

Some people were afraid Tommy's party would take away their freedom or their right to do business. A group of oil, mining and manufacturing companies got together to fight the CCF.

But Tommy was a wonderful speaker: funny, sincere and charming. He used a story called "Mouseland" to explain what the CCF was trying to do. He compared Canada to a country of little mice that foolishly elected cats to rule them. Tommy said, "Presently there came along one little mouse who had an idea. . . . And he said to the other mice, 'Look, fellows, why do we keep on electing a government made up of cats? Why don't we elect a government made up of mice?'"

His Mouseland story made people laugh, and it made them think. The type of government Tommy was proposing is called democratic socialism, and it had never been tried in North America. It promised to give farmers and other workers everything they'd wished for: electricity and indoor plumbing, paved roads, secure jobs and — of course — medical care.

How would Tommy's government pay for all of this? He promised that it could be done, and people trusted him. One reporter said, "Douglas doesn't have to kiss babies. Babies kiss him." He won by a landslide. Tommy and his team rolled up their sleeves. It was time for more guts and determination. They threw themselves into the work. And, boy oh boy, did they succeed. They passed more than one hundred new laws. Up went the power lines and telephone poles. Down went the outhouses and *flush* went the new toilets as people got indoor plumbing. Cars whizzed down the newly paved roads. Tommy's team spent more than two-thirds of its budget on doctors, schools and help for peo-ple who didn't have jobs. And that wasn't all. In just two years, using brains and talent and sheer stubbornness, Tommy's new government paid off $20 million of Sas-katchewan's debt.

Did people like what Tommy was doing? Did they elect him again? And again?

You'd better believe it!

Sixteen years passed. The province's debt kept going down. Roads and schools and all the other services kept get-ting better and better. But there was still one thing that both-ered Tommy. Can you guess what it was?

Yes, you are absolutely right. It was medical care. Rich people could afford to pay for good doctors. Poor people could not.

Finally, in 1960, Premier Tommy decided his province was ready for a new — and shocking — idea. He called it Medicare. It would give free medical care to patients in hos-pitals. But that wasn't all. Medicare would also cover visits to doctors and clinics. The government would pay for all of it.

Doctors and health insurance companies hated the idea. They were scared of losing money. They were afraid the gov-ernment would interfere with their work and take away patients' rights. They spent more than $100,000 on a cam-paign to convince people that Medicare was a bad idea. But the campaign didn't work. Once again Tommy won the elec-tion with a big majority. His dream was finally going to come true. Medicare was really going to happen.

But first there was a fight.

Medicare came in, but the doctors went out. They went on

strike. They shouted and held rallies and refused to work. They argued that Medicare would endanger people's privacy and even their lives.

During the strike one child's parents drove around desperately looking for medical help. But it was too late. The child died.

Still, the doctors stuck to their guns. And Tommy stuck to *his* guns. The bitter fight lasted more than three weeks. Finally, after twenty-three days, the doctors surrendered and went back to work. Tommy promised that Medicare would succeed. He said it would work so well that all the other provinces would follow Saskatchewan's example. He was right.

Around this time, a new political party was born. It was called the NDP, which stands for New Democratic Party, and guess who was chosen as its first leader? Yes, his name started with *T* and ended with *ommy*. As leader of the new party, **THE GREATEST CANADIAN** went back into federal politics — back to Ottawa.

That was the start of a tough time for Tommy. Things had changed. As the years went by, he began to realize that voters didn't love him as much as they used to. The doctors' strike had hurt his image, and his shiny new ideas were commonplace now. As if that weren't bad enough, **THE GREATEST CANADIAN** was running against the hottest new candidate in Canada: Pierre Trudeau. Young, handsome, brilliant and funny, Trudeau won the election by a big majority and became the prime minister. Tommy stayed in government as the leader of the NDP.

But he wasn't done yet. In 1970 trouble came to Canada,

and Tommy had to stand up for his beliefs again. In Quebec, a terrorist group called the Front de liberation du Québec (FLQ) kidnapped two politicians. The terrorists wanted Quebec to stop being a Canadian province and have a separate government from the rest of Canada. Canadians were shocked. Nobody knew how many terrorists there were, or where they were hiding, or what they might do.

Such a thing had never happened before, and everyone was very scared. To deal with the emergency, the prime minister wanted to use a law called the War Measures Act. It would mean the government could call in the army, search people or arrest them without a warrant and keep them in jail without laying any charges against them.

Tommy stood alone against this plan. He accused the prime minister of "using a sledgehammer to crack a peanut." Tommy and fifteen other members of his party voted against the plan, but they lost badly. At the time, few people agreed with Tommy, especially after one of the kidnapped politicians, Pierre Laporte, was found dead in the trunk of his car.

The army policed the streets with tanks, guns and helicopters. More than 450 people were arrested and sent to jail without trial. Only 20 of them were charged with crimes. Finally the murderers were caught and sent to prison, and the FLQ disbanded.

Later, Canadians decided to change the War Measures Act. It was replaced with a new law called the Emergencies Act, which gives the government extra rights — but not *too* much power — for dealing with special emergencies. This change didn't happen until after **THE GREATEST CANADIAN** had died, but I think he would have been pleased. Don't you?

I must say that the loss of my briefcase feels like a special emergency. It doesn't seem to be here in the T.C. Douglas Building, so let's go outside and sit on the grass while I help you work on your essays.

Tommy retired from politics in 1979. Then the honours started rolling in. This big building, with its art gallery and meadow stretching down to the water, was named after him. For his "new initiatives in the arts, health, industry, road building, energy and justice" he was made a Companion of the Order of Canada. In 1985 he received the Saskatchewan Order of Merit.

When he was eighty-one, Tommy died of cancer. His gravestone says, *Courage my friends, 'tis not too late to make a better world.*

In 1998 he was inducted into the Canadian Medical Hall of Fame for making a health care system that "remains as a model and source of envy to other countries around the world." And then, six years later, in a huge coast-to-coast-to-coast contest, Canadians voted him the you know what. Yes! **THE GREATEST CANADIAN!** Wouldn't Tommy have been thrilled?

But now we must hurry back to the big black taxi and on to our next stop. You've got assignments to write. And I don't want my briefcase to fall into the wrong hands!

Just the Plain Facts about Tommy Douglas

October 20, 1904
Tommy Douglas was born in Falkirk, Scotland.

1910 His father immigrated to Winnipeg, Manitoba. The rest of the family arrived in 1911.

1914 A visiting surgeon performed a lifesaving operation on Tommy's leg, free of charge.

1914–1919
> World War I. The family returned to Scotland, but in 1919 they came back to Canada.

June 21, 1919
> He and a friend witnessed "Bloody Saturday" during the Winnipeg General Strike.

1924–1933
> He attended Brandon College in Manitoba, and then studied at McMaster University and the University of Chicago.

1930 He married Irma Dempsey. They had one daughter, named Shirley, who became a Hollywood actress. Later they adopted a second daughter, Joan.

1931 He became a minister in Weyburn, Saskatchewan.

1935 He joined the CCF (Co-Operative Commonwealth Federation) and became a federal Member of Parliament.

1941 When the party's leader went to fight in World War II, Tommy replaced him as the leader of the Saskatchewan CCF party. Tommy had been refused for military service because of his old leg injury.

1944 He led the CCF party to a landslide victory in a provincial election and became premier of Saskatchewan.

October 13, 1961
> He introduced the Saskatchewan Medical Care Insurance Act.

1961 The CCF merged with some labour unions to form a new party called the NDP (New Democratic Party). Tommy was its first leader.

1962 He lost the federal election, partly because of the continuing controversy over Medicare. However, after winning a by-election he continued to serve in the federal government.

1970 He opposed the use of the War Measures Act in Quebec during the FLQ crisis.

1971 He resigned as leader of the NDP but continued in the federal government as its energy critic.

1979 He retired. He and his wife lived in the Gatineau Hills near Ottawa. He devoted his retirement years to reforestation, planting new trees on his property.

1981 He was made a Companion of the Order of Canada.

1985 He received the Saskatchewan Order of Merit.

February 24, 1986
  He died of cancer and was buried in Ottawa.

1998 He was inducted into the Canadian Medical Hall of Fame.

2004 Canadians voted him "The Greatest Canadian" in a CBC television contest.

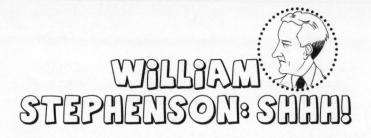

WiLLiAM STEPHENSON: SHHH!

One thing we learn from the lives of famous Canadians is that they *never give up*. We won't give up, either. Nothing will stop us from finding my lost briefcase — or from writing a first-rate essay. Please turn up your collars and make sure you have your spy notebooks. We're going to Intrepid Park in Whitby, Ontario. Intrepid means "brave" or "fearless." It certainly describes the man we're going to learn about now.

Many things about William Stephenson are a mystery. His life was full of secrets. For a long time, historians thought he was born on January 11, 1896, into a Scottish family named Stephenson. But he wasn't. A researcher found out that Bill was really born on January 23, 1897, to an Icelandic/British family named Stanger. When Bill was four, his father died and his mother moved away. Bill was raised by another Icelandic family whose name had been changed to Stephenson.

Bill grew up in Winnipeg. As a teenager he worked for a telegraph company — first delivering telegrams on his bike and later keying messages into telegraph machines. He didn't know it then, but when he grew up he'd be sending a lot more telegrams — most of them in secret code.

Let's park the taxi here. I'll apply my false moustache and sunglasses, and you can bring your spy cameras. Feel free to snap photos of this concrete monument with the flags flying over it.

Welcome to Camp X. During World War II, this was a school for secret agents. It's just an empty field now, stretching down to Lake Ontario. But from 1941 to 1944, there were houses, roads and transmission towers here. More than two thousand agents were trained here, and thousands of secret messages flowed through this place every day. The man in charge of it all was Bill Stephenson.

How did he go from delivering telegrams to running the biggest spy operation in the Western world? Well, it started with a plane crash, a narrow escape and a can opener.

During World War I, Bill was a flying ace. He flew a Sopwith Camel biplane. One day he saw a French plane being attacked by some German planes. Zooming to the rescue, he fought them back, but in the confusion his plane was shot down. He survived the crash but was wounded and captured by Germans. He spent the rest of the war in a prisoner-of-war camp.

Life in the camp was so boring that Bill began to make up dangerous little games for himself — sneaking around and stealing small objects from the guards. Once he stole a photograph. Another time he stole a can opener.

It wasn't just any can opener. To use it, you clamped the can between two handles and turned a crank to slice off the lid. Nowadays this is a common item. Maybe you have one in your kitchen. But during World War I it was a brand-new model — not available in North America. Bill was thrilled. If he patented that can opener, he could insult the Germans and make lots of money at the same time. There was just one small problem. First he would have to escape from the prison camp.

We don't know exactly how he did it, but he did. Soon after the war ended he was home in Winnipeg, manufacturing and selling hardware and car parts . . . and Kleen Kut can openers. Few people knew that their can-opener salesman was a decorated war hero.

Everyone who met him noticed Bill's quiet way of moving and talking. Later he became known as "the Quiet Canadian." But he was extremely alert and noticed everything around him. If you told him something, he would listen silently and then answer in a few words. He never bragged or drew attention to himself in any way.

I'm sorry to say that his hardware business lasted only about a year. Soon he owed money to a lot of people, and he couldn't pay. Time for another daring escape!

Bill slipped away to Britain, where he made friends with a man who was an expert in communications technology. Together they invented a way to send pictures through telephone wires: an early form of the fax machine. Then they learned how to send the pictures through radio signals (Look, Ma. No wires!) and in 1924 the *London Daily Mail* newspaper printed one — the first wireless photo ever sent.

Bill could imagine what was coming next. The process of sending the photos would get faster and faster. And a series of photos sent one after the other, very quickly, would appear to move. Movies! Television! Bill invested money in these new technologies and in some other companies as well.

He became a millionaire. He made friends with important people. He married a beautiful woman from a rich and important American family. Things were looking up for the Quiet Canadian.

But trouble was rumbling in Europe. In Germany, Adolf Hitler was planning to conquer many countries. Bill often visited Germany, where his work took him into important factories and meetings. He could see plenty of evidence that Hitler was getting ready to fight. Bill gave the evidence to a British member of parliament named Winston Churchill.

Churchill tried to warn the British prime minister, but at that time many countries — including Britain — were still recovering from the shock of World War I. They didn't want to think about getting into another war. Nobody wanted to challenge Hitler. So over the next few years, Hitler captured one territory after another without a fight. Each time, he lied and said he wouldn't do it again. But by 1939 the other countries finally realized he wouldn't stop. War was coming.

The British secret service began listening to coded messages that were being sent by their enemies. A brilliant group of code-breakers was hired to work in a secret hideout in England called Bletchley Park. The group included mathematicians, chess experts, crossword puzzle champions and scientists.

The Germans had a machine called Enigma, which could

send messages in a code that was almost unbreakable. Almost . . . but not quite! The British got hold of an Enigma machine and, over the course of the war, the Bletchley Park code-breakers figured out how to use it. From then on they were able to listen to German messages. They could find out where the enemy might strike next.

Only a few people in the world were allowed to know about Bletchley Park and Enigma. Bill Stephenson was one of them.

On September 1, 1939, Hitler invaded Poland. For Britain this was the last straw. War broke out. But Britain didn't have enough ships, planes or soldiers to win a war against Hitler. They desperately needed help from the Americans. Meanwhile, the Americans desperately needed a secret service organization like the ones Britain had. The two countries decided to work together. Bill was sent to New York City to set up a big secret service project.

He soon became the Head of British Security Co-ordination, and the code name for his office was "Intrepid." Later, people used "Intrepid" as a nickname for Bill himself. Of course, the whole operation was top secret. The sign on the door said *British Passport Control.* Visitors never guessed that behind the scenes, twenty-four hours a day, hundreds of workers — most of them Canadian women — were intercepting messages, breaking enemy codes and planning top-secret missions.

Bill worked without pay, and even paid many of the organization's expenses himself. His job was to find out what the enemy was doing (and planning!). Bill personally carried top-secret messages between Winston Churchill, who had

just become the prime minister of Britain, and Franklin Delano Roosevelt, the president of the United States, acting as their go-between and adviser. He also started an organization that became the Central Intelligence Agency. (Maybe you've heard of it. It's usually called the CIA.)

Between missions, Bill recruited staff to intercept, decode, track and distribute thousands of secret messages all over the Western hemisphere. Some of his employees forged documents, trained spies and sneaked behind enemy lines. Others were assigned to protect British and American factories against sabotage. Many of his secret agents also worked in the field.

No, I don't mean *this* field, here in Intrepid Park, although many of them did get their training here. "In the field" means that agents sometimes spied on people outside the office or in foreign countries. Some of these adventures turned up later in spy novels. One of Bill's agents was Ian Fleming, who later wrote novels about a secret agent called James Bond. Fleming said James Bond was partly based on "a true spy . . . William Stephenson." Another of Bill's agents was Roald Dahl, who wrote the book *Charlie and the Chocolate Factory*. (History does not record whether Willie Wonka was based on the life of Bill, although they both had secret organizations and similar first names!)

In 1941 Japanese pilots attacked the United States by bombing the American military base at Pearl Harbor, in Hawaii. After that the United States could no longer stay on the sidelines. It joined the war.

By a strange coincidence, Bill's Camp X began operating just one day before the Japanese attack on Pearl Harbor. Over the next four years, more than two thousand British, Canadian and American secret agents were schooled here. (But I don't think they had to do assignments about famous Canadians for their teachers!) They learned to observe, to hide, to kill and to disguise themselves. They learned to blow things up and build something from nothing. They learned to climb and parachute. Many agents were sent on secret missions behind enemy lines. Some of them came back alive. Some of them died or disappeared.

Camp X played another crucial role in the war — it was a listening post. Bill bought a transmitter tower from an American radio station and installed it here. Secret messages were received, decoded and forwarded to people in the intelligence services called BSC, CIA, COI, FBI, OSS, OWI, RCMP,

SIS and SOE. (Good grief — all those initials sound like a secret code. Can you break it?)* Because so many people were in charge of this huge project, it was named after a many-headed creature from Greek mythology: Hydra. Toward the end of the war, Hydra received more than nine thousand messages and sent thirty thousand messages every day.

Bill's experts worked feverishly to decode the enemy messages. Some of the codes were very complex and depended on special machines. Others were simpler. In one code, the sender and receiver each used a copy of the same book. Instead of writing a word, the sender wrote where it appeared in the book. For example, *52-3-2* meant "Look on page 52, line 3, the second word." If you didn't know which book was being used, you couldn't break the code.

Meanwhile, the Germans were still using their Enigma machines for top-secret messages. They didn't realize the code had been broken. Actually, thanks to computer experts at Camp X, Enigma messages could be decoded faster than ever. Naturally the Camp X computer had to be kept super-, mega-, *ultra*-secret. It was called ULTRA.

Near the end of the war, ULTRA was used to lure the Germans away from the beach at Normandy, where a big attack was being planned. The Allies decided to fool the Germans by setting up a fake invasion somewhere else. But would it work? They waited in terrible suspense. Suddenly

*British Security Co-ordination, Central Intelligence Agency, Coordinator of Information, Federal Bureau of Investigation, Office of Strategic Services, Office of War Information, Royal Canadian Mounted Police, Secret Intelligence Service, Special Operations Executive.

an agent came running into the room with an ULTRA message. Hitler was sending tanks and troops to the *wrong* beach. The trick had succeeded! The D-Day invasion at Normandy was still one of the bloodiest battles in history, but the Allies' plan worked. The Germans began to retreat.

On April 30, 1945, Hitler killed himself in his hideout in Germany. A week later Bill was in New York when the message arrived that Germany had surrendered. The Allies had won! All over the Western world, people celebrated VE (Victory in Europe) Day. Bill spent the day writing thank-you letters to his staff. A few months later, after the Allies dropped atomic bombs on two Japanese cities, Japan surrendered and the war ended.

To honour Bill's work, the British made him a knight. He became Sir William Stephenson. From the Americans he received the Presidential Medal of Freedom, the highest award a non-military person can get. Bill was the first non-American to get it. Later the Canadians made him a Member of the Order of Canada. When a new college was built for Canada's spy agency, the Canadian Security Intelligence Service (CSIS — pronounce it like this: SEE-siss), they named it the Sir William Stephenson Academy.

In spite of all these honours and the books that were written about him, Bill spent the rest of his life quietly. He worked in business in the West Indies and retired to Bermuda. He lived to be ninety-two years old and died in 1989.

Late in his life, and after his death, experts squabbled about who William Stephenson really was, what he really did and what really happened in his life. They are still trying to work out the details. We'll never know very much about his secret work during the war. Thousands of papers and files were burned afterward. The agents who survived the war kept quiet about their work. And many of the records are still kept secret by the British, Canadian and American governments.

But while the experts may argue about the details, they all agree on one thing. As you follow me into the field where Camp X once stood, please write it in your spy notebooks:

> ## YROO DZH ZM ZNZARMT NZM.
> ## SV SVOKVW GL DRM GSV DZI.**

**Can you break the code? Perhaps this will come in handy:

A	B	C	D	E	F	G	H	I	J	K	L	M	N	O	P	Q	R	S	T	U	V	W	X	Y	Z
z	y	x	w	v	u	t	s	r	q	p	o	n	m	l	k	j	i	h	g	f	e	d	c	b	a

P.S. Hint: *Yroo* stands for *Bill*. Can you decode the rest of the message now?

P.P.S. Don't worry! Even the experts sometimes get stuck. To find the answer, look at the bottom of page 90.

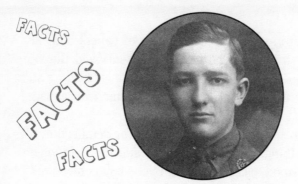

FACTS
FACTS
FACTS

Just the Plain Facts about William Stephenson

January 23, 1897
William Samuel Clouston Stanger was born.

1901 His father died. His mother couldn't raise three children on her own, so her friends the Stephensons raised Bill.

1916 When World War I broke out, he enlisted in the army.

1916 He was wounded by poison gas.

1917 When he recovered, he became a fighter pilot.

1918 He shot down more than twelve enemy planes and won several medals before being shot down and captured by the Germans.

1918 He escaped the prisoner-of-war camp and made his way home to Winnipeg.

1921 He moved to London, England, where he and a friend invented a forerunner of the fax machine and a device for sending photographs through radio waves.

July 22, 1924
He married an American named Mary Simmons.

1936 He informed British MP Winston Churchill that Adolf Hitler had secretly spent more than £800 million to build up its armed forces. Churchill tried to warn the British prime minister about the Nazi threat.

September 1, 1939
Hitler invaded Poland, triggering World War II.

1940 Winston Churchill, who had recently become the prime minister of Britain, sent Bill to New York City. Bill was in charge of British Security Co-ordination in the Western hemisphere.

December 6, 1941
Camp X opened. It was the first training school for secret agents in North America.

December 7, 1941
Japan attacked the United States at Pearl Harbor, and the United States joined the war.

May 7, 1945
Germany surrendered. The Allies celebrated Victory in Europe Day.

August 1945
The Allies dropped atomic bombs on the cities of Hiroshima and Nagasaki. A few weeks later, the Japanese surrendered and World War II ended.

1945 Bill became Sir William Stephenson. On the paper that recommended him for knighthood, Winston Churchill wrote, *This one is dear to my heart.*

1946 In the U.S., he received the Presidential Medal of Freedom.

1980 He became a Member of the Order of Canada.

January 31, 1989
He died in Bermuda.

DR. BETHUNE FIGHTS SOME GERMS

Please stay together and wait for my signal to cross the street toward the Guy-Concordia Metro Station. The Montreal traffic is going every which way. Be careful! *Faites attention! Merci!*

It won't take long to search for my briefcase here. Please spread out and look for clues. But don't touch anything. There are a lot of pigeons and a lot of germs. While you're searching, I'll tell you about the man on this statue. He was a famous Canadian who had some extraordinary adventures and an early death, all because of germs.

His name was Henry Norman Bethune, but people called him Norman. He was a restless kid from a strict family. He was born in Gravenhurst, Ontario, but his family moved seven times while Norman was growing up. Everywhere they went, he got into trouble. His father tried to settle him down — sometimes harshly — but Norman just wasn't the settling-down type.

After high school, Norman became a teacher in a small Ontario town. Then he went to university. Then he changed his mind and became a lumberjack and teacher in a lumber camp. Then he went back to university to study medicine. Then war broke out.

Oh, dear. It's starting to rain. There's a Chinese restaurant down the street where we can take shelter with tea and fortune cookies. Hurry! As soon as we're settled, I'll continue.

Whew! We made it. Please take a seat.

There, are you all set? Let's each order a different dish and then share. Do you know how to eat with chopsticks?

When World War I broke out, Norman joined up right away. He went to the battlefield as a stretcher-bearer. One day, while he was carrying a wounded soldier to safety, a German bomb exploded. Pieces of the bomb hit Norman's leg. It was a bad injury. It took him six months to recover. Afterward he was sent back to Toronto to finish his medical studies.

Around this time, a young woman approached Norman in the street and gave him a white feather.

Pardon? No, indeed. It didn't mean she liked Norman. The white feather was an insult. It meant "Why haven't you joined the army, you coward?" It was supposed to shame people into enlisting. But of course Norman didn't deserve it. (Many people feel that *nobody* deserved it, and that the whole white feather campaign was cruel.)

As soon as he graduated, Norman went

back to the fighting — first as a surgeon in the British navy and then in France until the war ended. In peacetime Norman was as intense and restless as ever. Studying medicine, he moved from England to Canada and back again.

Then he fell in love with a young woman named Frances Campbell Penney. She was much younger than he was. Her family wasn't thrilled when the two lovebirds ran away and got married.

And how do you think things went after that?
Do you think:
(a) It was all butterflies, moonlight and happy picnics in the park.
(b) It involved noisy fights, tears, broken dishes and broken hearts.

After the wedding Norman said, "Now I can make your life a misery, but I'll never bore you."

Perhaps you can guess where this sad tale is going. Frances had inherited some money from her uncle, but she and Norman spent it zooming all over Europe on a six-month honeymoon. The next thing they knew, they were living in Detroit, struggling to make ends meet. This was not the most fun they had ever had. And things were about to get worse.

Norman caught tuberculosis. It was caused by germs, probably from his contact with sick patients, and it got into his left lung. Nowadays, vaccines can prevent the disease and drugs can treat it. But in those days the usual treatment was fresh air, good food and months or years of rest. Even people who could afford this treatment sometimes died. For poor people the diagnosis was almost a death sentence.

Norman went away to a kind of hospital called a sanatorium near a beautiful lake in the woods. But do you think he was a nice, obedient, easygoing patient? No way. He had parties with his friends. He smoked cigarettes. He argued with his doctors about a new treatment that could either cure him or kill him. He argued until they gave in, and to everyone's surprise, the risky operation worked. A couple of months later, Norman was cured. He left the sanatorium healthy, and determined to help other patients.

In the meantime, he and Frances had gotten a divorce. Norman threw himself into his work and — as usual — moved often. First he worked at a tuberculosis hospital in New York State. Then he moved here to Montreal and became an expert in chest surgery at the Royal Victoria Hospital and later at the Sacré Coeur Hospital north of Montreal. In his spare time he set up a free clinic for people who didn't have jobs. He organized, and paid for, free art classes for children in his apartment. He invented new medical instruments and wrote articles about new surgical techniques.

Norman was energetic and impatient and hard to get along with. If he didn't like a piece of equipment, he would throw it across the operating room. If he didn't agree with someone, he would say so. Loudly.

In 1929, he and Frances got married again! If you think they lived happily ever after, please raise your chopsticks. If you think the old fights and unhappiness soon started up again, please shake your heads sadly. I'm sorry to say you are right. Their second divorce happened in 1933. After that Norman took a trip to the Soviet Union — a trip that changed his life. He was amazed and excited by the medical system there. For years he had been saying that tuberculosis could be avoided if patients got good medical care, no matter whether they were rich or poor. In Canada and the United States, nobody took his idea seriously. But in the Soviet Union he saw proof that he was right. In just twenty years, the number of tuberculosis cases there had been cut in half. Norman went straight home and tried to set up a similar system in Canada.

What do you think happened? Do you think:
(a) Everyone cheered and carried him around on their shoulders.
(b) Nothing. They ignored him.

Yes. His idea fell flat. In the 1930s Canadians weren't ready for the idea of government-paid medical care. Doctors wanted to go on being paid directly by their patients. And most Canadians were dead set against anything that reminded them of Communism. In a Communist system, everyone is supposed to share work and property (and important services, like medical care) equally. But most Canadians felt that Communism would take away their freedom. They wanted nothing to do with it.

Norman disagreed. He became a Communist.

Around this time a civil war broke out in Spain. A dictator named Francisco Franco was trying to take control of the country. Canada passed a law that made it illegal for Canadians to join either side in the Spanish Civil War, but Norman — and 1200 others — ignored the law. They went to fight against Franco.

In Spain, bombs and guns were killing thousands of people. Injured people were dying because it took too long to get to the hospital. Norman knew that many could be saved with blood transfusions — if the blood could be given quickly enough. He started collecting blood from healthy people in the city of Madrid and sending it to the battlefields, where it could be given to wounded people on the spot. It was the first mobile blood transfusion service in the world, and it was a huge success. Soon the number of deaths went down by as much as seventy-five percent.

But the hard work and strain seemed to make Norman more impatient than ever. He argued with the Spanish doctors. He argued with his friends. He argued with the Communist Party. Soon he left Spain.

Two years after that, Franco won the war. He took control of Spain in 1939 and stayed in power until 1975. But Norman would never know this. (Uh-oh. Can you guess why? I'm afraid it starts with *g* and ends with *erms*. But let's not jump ahead to that awful part of the story just yet.)

Back in Canada, Norman travelled everywhere, lecturing about the Spanish war and collecting money to help the people there. Partway through this tour he heard about another war. Japan had invaded China, and the Chinese Communist army was fighting against the invaders in the northern mountains. Right away, Norman wanted to help.

He sailed for China. A nurse who spoke fluent Chinese went with him as an interpreter. For several months they gave medical care to people in different Chinese towns. Then Mao Zedong, the leader of the Communist army, asked to meet with Norman. (Later Mao would become the leader of all the Chinese people. But Norman would never hear about that because . . . well, you know. Brace yourselves.)

They met in a cave where Mao was living. The two men talked all night. Norman hoped to use his mobile blood transfusion service again, but this time it wouldn't work. The roads were too rough. There was no electricity. The donated blood couldn't be cooled. Instead, Norman and his team put together loads of medical supplies that could be carried by mules. Then they headed toward the fighting. The suffering they saw was terrible. There were only a few doctors to serve the soldiers and the civilians in that region — all 13 million of them!

Norman and his team quickly trained others to help with first aid and even to do simple operations. They set up more

than twenty hospitals. And they did plenty of doctoring themselves. One time Norman operated on 115 people in a row. He refused to stop until the last patient was taken care of — sixty-nine hours later! Word spread quickly about this amazing doctor. People loved him not just for his medical skills, but also because he shared everything he had with those who needed it — even his food and clothes.

Norman was working harder than he had ever worked in his life, and that's really saying something. But here comes the sad part. One day when he was operating with his bare hands (because there were no surgical gloves), his scalpel slipped. He cut his finger. Ow!

He stuck the injured finger in some iodine — DOUBLE OW! — and finished the operation. Norman thought everything would be fine. After all, this wasn't the first time he had cut himself.

But it wasn't all right. His hand swelled up. Then his whole arm. Germs had gotten into the cut and were spreading through his body. In Canada there were drugs to take care of an infection like that, but Norman wasn't in Canada. The infection got worse and worse.

Norman knew he was dying. He wrote a letter stating his final wishes. At the end of the letter he wrote, *The last two years have been the most significant, the most meaningful years of my life.*

Then he died.

It was incredibly sad. Ten thousand people filed past his coffin. He was buried in Chu-ch'eng, but the Japanese invaded, and Norman's body was taken to a safer place.

Now he is buried in the Cemetery of Martyrs in the city of Shijiazhuang, across the road from a beautiful hospital called the Norman Bethune International Peace Hospital. In the cemetery is a statue of Norman that looks exactly like the one we've just visited here in Montreal.

Many statues of Norman can be found in China. He is even more famous there than he is in Canada. When Mao Zedong became the leader of China, he wrote an essay that told what a hero Norman was, and how he had given his life to serve others. During the late 1960s, every person in China was required to read that essay. No wonder Norman is famous there!

Here in Canada we also honour him. The house where he was born is now a national museum. In 1972 he was named a Person of National Historic Significance. And on the hundredth anniversary of his birth, both Canada and China issued postage stamps with pictures of Norman on them.

Well, that was a sad ending. And I'm sad to say that our delicious Chinese meal is finished, too. To cheer ourselves up, let's compare the fortunes from our fortune cookies. What does yours say? *Your teacher will give you an excellent mark on your assignment.* Congratulations!

Look! Mine says, *You will soon find the thing you seek.* Do you think it means I'll find my briefcase? Oh, I hope so! Let's go back to the big black taxi and continue our trip backward through my previous Historical Excursion™. As we hurry past the statue of Norman Bethune, please stop for a moment. Bow respectfully.

Now jump in! We're off to our next stop!

Just the Plain Facts about Norman Bethune

March 3, 1890

Norman Bethune was born in Gravenhurst, Ontario. While he was growing up, his family moved to several different towns in Ontario.

1909–1912
He began to study medicine, but stopped for two years to become a lumberjack/teacher at Frontier College.

1912 He continued his medical studies at the University of Toronto.

1914 When World War I broke out, he enlisted.

1915 While serving as a stretcher-bearer in France, he was badly wounded. He spent six months recovering. Then he was sent back to Canada to finish his medical studies.

1916 He graduated and joined the British Royal Navy, serving as a ship's surgeon.

1918 When the war ended, he moved from England to Canada and back again, continuing his medical studies.

August 13, 1923
He married Frances Campbell Penney. After a six-month honeymoon in Europe, they moved to Detroit, Michigan.

1926 He contracted pulmonary tuberculosis and went to a sanatorium at Saranac Lake in upstate New York.

1927 He insisted that his doctors perform a risky operation on his lung. Seven weeks later he was well enough to leave the sanatorium. He and Frances divorced.

1928–1935
He specialized in chest surgery at the Royal Victoria Hospital in Montreal and later at the Sacré-Coeur Hospital in Cartierville, Quebec. He also set up a free clinic for the unemployed in Montreal and organized free art classes for children in his Montreal

apartment. He and Frances married again in 1929 and divorced in 1933.

1935 He visited the Soviet Union and admired the medical system there. He joined the Communist Party and tried without success to introduce the idea of free medicare in Canada.

October 1936
He went to help in the Spanish Civil War and organized the first-ever mobile blood transfusion service. The number of deaths among the wounded went down by as much as seventy-five percent.

1937 He returned to Canada, where he gave lectures and raised money to aid Spain.

July 7, 1937
The Japanese army invaded China. The Chinese Communist army, led by Mao Zedong, fought to stop the invasion.

January 1938
He sailed to China to help Mao's army.

March 1938
He met with Mao Zedong to talk about medical care for those fighting in the remote northern region of China.

1938–1939
He travelled into the northern mountains, where the fighting was fierce. There were few doctors to care for millions of people in the region. He taught medics and nurses, and organized more than twenty hospitals.

October 1939
While operating on a wounded soldier, he cut his hand with a scalpel. The wound became infected.

November 12, 1939
> He died at Huang Shiko, in northern China.

1966–1969
> During China's Cultural Revolution, everyone in the People's Republic of China was required to read three essays. One of them was Mao Zedong's essay on Norman Bethune. Today in China, Norman is still honoured as a great hero.

1972 In Canada, he was named a Person of National Historic Significance.

1990 To celebrate the hundredth anniversary of Norman's birth, Canada and China issued two postage stamps in his honour.

1998 He was inducted into the Canadian Medical Hall of Fame.

ARCHIE BELANEY (GREY OWL): A CAUTIONARY TALE

Our motorboat ride across Lake Ajawaan is over. Please take off your life jackets. We'll walk the rest of the way to Grey Owl's cabin. Today's field trip is full of danger, so stick together. Listen to my warnings. And please remember to look for my briefcase along the way.

In the spring of 1938, Grey Owl came home for the last time. He was too tired to walk, so someone drove him across the ice in a car. (**Danger!** Never do that! Your car could fall through the ice!) But a few days later he fell sick with pneumonia and was taken to the hospital in Prince Albert, Saskatchewan, where he died. He was fifty years old. He was famous. And shortly after his death, the world found out the shocking truth about him.

Grey Owl was *not* the native person he had pretended to be. He was Archibald Stansfeld Belaney. Born in England in 1888 and raised by his prim and proper English aunts, young Archie spent a lot of time getting into trouble.

The worst trouble came when he was a teenager, working as a clerk in a lumberyard. One day he lit a package of fireworks. (**Danger!** Never, ever, play with fireworks!) He lowered them down the chimney into his supervisor's office and . . .

BOOM!

Luckily nobody was killed or injured. But that was the end of *that* job!

Archie had always dreamed of living in the woods. After the fireworks incident, his aunts finally let him come to Canada, where he got a job in a Toronto department store. (**Danger!** . . . Just kidding. Department stores are not usually dangerous.) A few months later, he began to follow his dream. He boarded a train and headed for northern Ontario.

Archie stayed with a family near Lake Temiskaming and learned about life in the bush. Then he got a job doing chores at the new tourist lodge on Temagami Island. Many of the other staff were Anishinabe (Ojibwa) people, and that suited Archie just fine. He was eager to learn their language and customs. They were kind to him and answered his questions patiently.

But Archie continued to get into **Trouble with a capital T.** You're too young to hear those details, so just write *danger* a few times in your notebook and turn the page.

Pardon? Did you say that your teacher will expect you to include the *facts* about his bad behaviour in your essay? Are you sure?

Oh, dear.

Well, when Archie went overseas to fight in World War I, he already had one wife and daughter. When he came back, he had a second wife, who didn't know about the first one. Meanwhile his baby son had been born to a third woman.

During the war Archie was wounded in the foot, and after that he was often in pain. When the war was over, he went back to Ontario, but his troubles continued. One of his wives divorced him. His son's mother died. Archie lived alone in the woods, drank too much alcohol (Ooh! **Danger!**) and practised dangerous stunts, such as throwing knives. (Don't even *think* about it!) He couldn't get a job. He was broke. He let his hair grow long, dyed it black and tied it in a ponytail. He started telling people that his father was Apache and his mother was Scottish.

His life became a tangle of lies.

Then he met a waitress from the local hotel. She was a clever and beautiful Kanien'kehaka (Mohawk) woman named Gertrude Bernard. Everyone called her Pony, but when she and Archie fell in love, he made up a new name for her: Anahareo.

Pony gave up her scholarship to an exclusive private school in Toronto and went to live with Archie in the woods. But when she saw what trappers did for a living, she was horrified. Archie clubbed animals and lifted their dead bodies out of the traps. Then he reset the traps. Pony scolded him for being so cruel, but Archie argued that if he stopped trapping, how would he make a living?

One day Pony found two orphaned baby beavers and brought them into the cabin. (**Danger!** Never pick up a wild animal, even a baby one! It could bite you. Or its mother could attack you.) Archie tried to ignore the babies, but one of them crawled up to nibble his eyebrows, let out a sigh and fell asleep on his chest.

"Well, I'll be darned!" said Archie.

The male beaver was called McGinnis and the female was McGinty, and they lived in the cabin with Archie and Pony. Do you think you could live like that — playing with the beavers and letting them sleep in your bed, scolding them when they chewed the legs off your table and covering a Christmas tree with treats for them — and still make your living as a trapper? Archie couldn't. Finally he said, "To kill such creatures seemed monstrous. I would do no more of it."

But without trapping, there wasn't enough money. Archie had a tiny pension from the army. He and Pony earned a little more by charging people 10¢ to see the beavers. She tried to make some money by prospecting for gold, and Archie wrote an essay about McGinnis and McGinty that was published in a magazine. But it still wasn't enough.

Then two good things happened. The magazine editors asked Archie to write a book. And Archie began speaking to audiences about the importance of preserving the wilderness. At first he was terrified. He felt "like a snake that has swallowed an icicle, chilled from one end to the other." But he gave wonderful speeches. People wanted to hear more.

Then . . . brace yourselves . . . something terrible happened. McGinnis and McGinty disappeared.

Please don't look at me like that. Archie and Pony searched everywhere for them. Maybe the beavers had been trapped. Maybe they went back to the wild to start families. Maybe they were kidnapped by aliens. (Sorry, that was a bad joke.) Anyway, they were never seen again.

After a while Archie and Pony adopted another beaver and called her Jelly Roll. While Pony went searching for gold in Quebec, Archie stayed home and wrote his book. When a mean otter started to bully Jelly, Archie felt he didn't have any choice — he set a trap for the otter. By accident he caught another young beaver! Its foot was injured and there was a cut on its head. Archie took it home and named it Rawhide. Rawhide was a laid-back, easygoing sort of beaver who seemed desperate for a friend. He stayed near Archie, slept in his bed and cried whenever Archie went out. At first bossy Jelly beat up the newcomer. But later she and Rawhide became great friends — and parents!

Archie's book was called *The Men of the Last Frontier*. It was about his adventures in the woods and the importance of preserving nature. This was a new theme for many readers, and the book quickly became a bestseller. He published it under his native name: Grey Owl. His readers, and the audiences at his lectures, had no idea that he was really an Englishman named Archie Belaney.

The Parks Service offered Grey Owl a job as its spokesperson, hiring him to appear in some films and to continue teaching people about nature. Archie and Pony moved to a national park in Manitoba, where Jelly and Rawhide became film stars. Audiences watched the beavers swimming, climbing into the canoe, drinking milk and cuddling up to Archie and Pony . . . or should I say, "Grey Owl and Anahareo." Jelly gave birth to four babies: Wakanee, Wakanoo, Silver Bells and Buckshot. But that year the lake was shallower than usual. There was a danger that it might freeze all the way to the bottom, and that would be terrible for the beavers. So the famous "family" moved here to Lake Ajawaan, in Saskatchewan.

Please be careful as we make our way down the hill to stand on the deck of Grey Owl's cabin. Inside you can see the beaver lodge where Jelly and Rawhide lived with their babies. The beavers could swim right up into the cabin through a tunnel under the water.

In this cabin Grey Owl wrote two more adult books, *Pilgrims of the Wild* and *Tales of an Empty Cabin*, and a children's book called *The Adventures of Sajo and Her Beaver People*. All three became bestsellers.

But if you think that Archie sat here quietly and calmly, writing and communing with nature, please think again. He struggled. He refused to take baths. He hated any kind of noise. He and Pony argued. Sometimes they got mean with each other. Meanwhile the beavers were constantly coming and going from the house. And visitors came from all over the world. The future prime minister, John Diefenbaker, came. So did the governor general.

Life got even busier when Pony gave birth to a baby girl. The baby's name was Dawn, and most of the time she lived in the city, where Pony and Archie visited her often. Sometimes Pony lived in town with her, and sometimes Dawn came to Lake Ajawaan. But Pony and Archie felt that Ajawaan was not a good place to raise a child. It was too remote. And Pony was sometimes away prospecting. So most of the time Dawn lived with a family in Prince Albert.

In 1935 Archie went to England to give lectures. "Grey Owl" promoted his book and delivered wonderful talks. Tickets sold out quickly, and extra performances were booked. He gave three or four shows a day. He was making a lot of money. And he was very tired.

With his long black hair, buckskin clothing and first-hand knowledge of nature, Archie appeared to be exactly what he said he was: First Nations. Very few white people doubted this. One scholar thought it was strange that Grey Owl greeted the audience in the language of a Plains tribe when he was supposed to be from the Eastern Woodlands. Another wondered why he wrote such flowery English prose. A newspaper reporter found out the truth about Archie three whole years before he died. And of course, many First Nations people knew what was going on. But nobody exposed him. Even the newspaper kept quiet.

Why? Because they respected Grey Owl's message. If Archie was exposed, people would feel cheated and angry. He wouldn't be able to give any more lectures about preserving the environment. No good would come from that. So everyone kept quiet.

But Archie was still Archie. He got married again — this time to a woman named Yvonne Perrier. He made some more films, gathered as much strength as he could and went back

to Britain for another tour. Once more he performed for sold-out audiences, giving two shows every day and three on Thursdays.

Near the end of 1937, he gave a Command Performance for the royal family and had tea with them at Buckingham Palace. Princess Elizabeth, who grew up to be our queen, said, "I wish I could go to Canada and see your beavers in their home."

By the time they got back to Canada, Archie and Yvonne were exhausted. Still they didn't stop. Archie toured for twelve more weeks, lecturing all over North America. As always, the audiences were huge and enthusiastic, but Archie's health got worse and worse. When they finally got back to Saskatchewan, Yvonne was admitted to hospital, but Archie was stubborn — he insisted on coming back here to the cabin. And . . . well, that brings us back to the beginning of our field trip. The park rangers drove him across the ice to this little cabin, but a few days later he died of pneumonia.

As soon as the North Bay *Nugget* heard about Grey Owl's death, it published the truth about him. The news quickly spread to other newspapers. The public was shocked. So was Pony. At first she couldn't believe it. She said, "I had the awful feeling for all those years I had been married to a ghost . . . and that Archie had never really existed."

In spite of the scandal, people still respected what Grey Owl stood for. Eight Canadian newspapers published editorials about him, but not one of them criticized him for lying. Today he is remembered as a pioneer in protecting the environment. So is Pony. Before she died, "Anahareo" was awarded the Order of Canada for her work in wilderness conservation.

Let's climb the ridge behind the cabin and visit the graves of Archie, Pony and Dawn. Feel free to explore. I know you will be careful and respectful — not like the rowdy group that was with me last time. I was so busy pulling them out of the lake and smothering fires that I didn't enjoy this peaceful setting at all. No wonder I lost my briefcase!

Just the Plain Facts about Archibald Belaney (Grey Owl)

September 18, 1888

Archibald Stansfeld Belaney was born in Hastings, England, and raised by his aunts, Ada and Carrie Belaney.

March 29, 1906

He moved to Canada to live in the wilderness. He lived with a family near Lake Temiskaming and learned about trapping and hunting.

1907–1908

He worked at the newly built Temagami Inn.

August 23, 1910

He married a young Anishinabe (Ojibwa) woman named Angele Egwuna. Her family called him Was-Sha-Quon-Asin, which means "White-Beaked Owl." Later he called himself "Grey Owl."

1911 He and Angele had a daughter named Agnes. When Agnes was two, he left them.

1913 He lived with a Métis woman named Marie Girard. (Her last name is sometimes spelled *Gerrard* or *Jero*.)

January 1915

He left Marie. In September she gave birth to his son, John. Marie soon died, and a kind neighbour raised the boy.

May 1915

He enlisted in the Canadian army.

June 1915

He was sent overseas.

April 23, 1916

While serving in Flanders (the Netherlands), he was wounded in the foot. He spent nearly a year recovering in England.

February 1917

He married an Englishwoman named Ivy Holmes.

September 1917

He returned to Canada. Before Ivy could join him, she learned of his marriage to Angele and divorced him.

1925 Back in Temagami, he behaved wildly. He was reunited with Angele but soon left again. He fell in love with a nineteen-year-old Kanien'kehaka (Mohawk) girl named Gertrude Bernard, whose nickname was Pony. "Grey Owl" called her "Anahareo."

Spring 1926

Angele gave birth to a daughter named Flora.

June 1926

He married Pony in an Anishinabe (Ojibwa) ceremony. She lived with him in the bush near Temagami. She thought trapping was cruel and urged him to give it up.

Spring 1928

He and Pony adopted two orphaned beavers and

called them McGinty and McGinnis. Archie gave up trapping and began to write and lecture about the importance of preserving wildlife.

1929 McGinty and McGinnis disappeared. Archie and Pony adopted a new beaver named Jelly Roll.

1929–1930
He wrote a book called *The Men of the Last Frontier*. While Pony was away on a trip, he adopted another beaver called Rawhide.

1931 *The Men of the Last Frontier* became a bestseller. The federal Parks Service hired "Grey Owl" to be its spokesman. He and "Anahareo" appeared in films with the beavers to educate the public about wilderness conservation.

October 1931
After a short time at Riding Mountain National Park in Manitoba, they moved to Prince Albert National Park in Saskatchewan.

August 23, 1932
He and Pony had a daughter named Dawn. Most of the time, she lived in town with a foster family named Winters.

1935 His new book, *Pilgrims of the Wild*, became a bestseller. "Grey Owl" went to England, where he gave more than 200 lectures to almost 500,000 people.

1936 He returned to Prince Albert to write his book, *Tales of an Empty Cabin*. Soon after it was published, Pony left him.

December 1936
He married a French-Canadian woman named Yvonne Perrier.

September 1937

>He and Yvonne went to Britain for another lecture tour.

December 10, 1937

>"Grey Owl" gave a Royal Command Performance at Buckingham Palace.

1938 He and Yvonne returned from England and gave a twelve-week lecture tour of North America to huge audiences.

April 13, 1938

>He died in Prince Albert, Saskatchewan. Soon after his death, the North Bay *Nugget* broke the news that "Grey Owl" was actually an Englishman named Archie Belaney.

SPEEDY TOM LONGBOAT

These roads may have changed a bit since 1900, but I don't think they've changed *too* much. Can you picture a thirteen-year-old boy running across that field, jumping over the fence and vanishing into the woodlot? Tom Longboat was supposed to be helping with chores, but he sneaked away to play lacrosse with his friends. His mother sent Tom's older brother to fetch him back, but the poor brother didn't stand a chance. Even as a young boy, Tom was unbelievably quick, and he could run incredibly far. That boy was born to run.

He grew up here, on the Six Nations Reserve near Brantford, Ontario. His Onondaga name was Cogwagee, which means "everything," and his English name was Tom Longboat. Before long he would be known as the fastest runner in the world!

When he was seventeen years old, Tom entered his first race — an 8-kilometre run that took place just down the road from here, in the town of Caledonia. He came second, and he loved the race. He loved competing. On the way home, Tom made up his mind to enter the race again next year — and to win. He began to train hard, running up and down these roads where our big black taxi is cruising.

The next year, Tom crossed the finish line 400 metres ahead of the next runner. After that there was no stopping him. He looked around for the next big race and began training harder than ever.

It was called the Around the Bay Race and it took place in Hamilton, Ontario, in October. The course was 30 kilometres long. Tom didn't have money for proper equipment, so he wore a sweatshirt, a pair of swimming trunks and cheap sneakers. When he stepped up to the starting line, people laughed, and when he began to run, they laughed even harder. In those days, runners held their arms up high and pumped their elbows as they raced. When Tom ran, he kept his arms low and relaxed. To the audience this looked ridiculous. But when he crossed the finish line a full three minutes ahead of everybody else, they stopped laughing and started asking each other, "Who is this guy?" From then on, he rarely saw the back of another runner. He was always **waaaaay out in front.**

In those days (and even now) there was one big race that serious runners dreamt of entering: the famous Boston Marathon. Tom wondered what it would feel like to pull **waaaaay out in front** of the others in such a big race. He began training at the West End YMCA in Toronto. Every day he lifted weights or played handball for an hour. A couple of times a week he did long runs and time trials. Between these sessions, he went for long walks. Nowadays athletes know that the best results come from intense workouts followed by "active rest," and that's exactly what Tom was doing. But in those days, athletes believed in working relentlessly, and Tom's recovery periods were considered laziness. He had to ignore a lot of bad advice and name-calling from coaches and promoters, but he stuck to the training system that worked for him.

And boy oh boy, did it work for him.

On April 19, 1907, Tom stood with 104 other runners at the starting line of the Boston Marathon. It was a cold, slushy day with a chilly breeze. At noon the starting gun was fired and the runners took off. In those days the course wound up and down some steep and difficult hills. After a couple of hours, some of Tom's toughest competitors collapsed from exhaustion. One runner got knocked down by a bicycle. About 13 kilometres from the finish line, Tom pulled into the lead. The police struggled to hold back the cheering crowd as he raced toward the finish line. Now and then Tom had to slow down to keep from bumping into an eager fan.

Victory! Tom won the race in 2 hours, 24 minutes and 24 seconds, beating the previous record by 5½ minutes. As soon as the race was over, he took a quick shower. Then he sat down to eat a steak dinner while other runners were still crossing the finish line. How did it feel to be **waaaaay out in front** of the others? Pretty darn good!

When Tom stepped off the train in Toronto, a huge crowd roared and cheered. They escorted him to City Hall in a torch-light parade and celebrated with fireworks. A gold medal was pinned to his chest, and the city announced that it would give him $500 to pay for his education. (It was a bit slow to pay up, though. The money wasn't handed over to Tom's family until 1980. With seventy-three years' worth of interest, it came to $10,000!)

Next stop . . . the Olympic Games. In 1908 the Games were held in London, England. The marathon was scheduled to start at Windsor Castle so the royal family could watch it without leaving home. They sat on thrones near the starting line. Young Edward VIII and George VI, who later became kings, watched eagerly. The weather was extremely hot as Tom and the other runners took their places near the royal family. The starting gun fired.

Off they went! (The runners, I mean. Not the royal family.) The course wound 42.2 kilometres through the streets of London to the Olympic stadium. After 27 kilometres (I feel tired just thinking about it) Tom was in second place. He wasn't **waaaaay out in front** yet. But he intended to be.

Uh-oh. All of a sudden, Tom slowed down and began to walk. Something was wrong. He seemed to pull himself together and ran for about 5 more kilometres. Then he suddenly stopped and fell to the ground. Medics carried him off the course. Poor Tom! He would never know how it felt to be **waaaaay out in front** of the other Olympic runners. He was out of the race!

What happened? Nobody knows for sure. Later in the race, another runner collapsed, and there were rumours that

he and Tom had taken drugs to make them run faster. Some people said Tom's manager had drugged Tom in order to win a bet. Other people thought the runners collapsed because of the extremely hot weather. The answer remains a mystery. (Much like the mystery of my lost briefcase.)

I'll turn the big black taxi into this scenic side road while I tell you about Tom's next adventure.

After his big disappointment at the Olympics, Tom gave up his amateur status but — like the other famous Canadians we've been learning about — he absolutely refused to quit. He became a professional runner, entering races all over North America and — yes — crossing the finish line **waaaaay ahead** of his competitors. Soon he entered the World's Professional Marathon Championship against an Italian runner named Dorando Pietri. (Pietri happened to be the other runner who had collapsed at the Olympics.) The race took place indoors at Madison Square Garden in New York City.

On the indoor track, 10 laps equalled 1 mile. That meant the race would be 262 laps long. The runners would have to go around and around, just as our big black taxi is going around and around in circles right now. What a funny road this is!

Dorando Pietri was smaller than Tom, and he was extra good at those tight turns. But Tom was better at the long straight parts. For most of the race the two runners were evenly matched. Then, suddenly, just six laps before the end, Pietri fell down, exhausted. Tom nearly tripped over him on his way to the finish line . . . but in the end, Tom finished **waaaaay out in front**, as usual.

His fans were thrilled. They cheered and whistled . . . just like those people who are yelling at us right now. Please wave at them as we go by.

The newspaper headline said *Longboat Retrieves His Olympic Defeat.* And things kept getting better and better for him. A couple of weeks later he married a beautiful Mohawk woman whose English name was Lauretta Maracle.

But Tom had plenty of struggles as well. He faced prejudice because of his First Nations heritage, and he was often treated unfairly. The newspapers even printed racist comments and nicknames. And Tom kept standing up to coaches who called him lazy. He knew his training system worked, but they still didn't understand it. They kept pushing him to "work harder."

The tension built. Out of the blue, Tom's trainer sold his contract to another trainer for $2000. Tom was shocked. "He sold me just like a racehorse," he said. A few months later, his contract was sold again — this time for $700. Now Tom was fed up. He bought his own contract and took charge of his training and promotion himself. People said it wouldn't work, but it did. Tom ran as successfully as ever.

And *we* are still whizzing around this funny circular road. Some speedy-looking cars have joined us and they all seem to be driving very fast. Please make sure your seatbelts are fastened.

When Tom was twenty-seven, World War I broke out. Tom was one of the 292 Six Nations men who joined up. He was sent to France as a dispatch runner, carrying important messages from one army post to another. It was dangerous work, and he was wounded twice.

Once he was even declared dead.

It happened when a shell blew up near a communications post where Tom was standing. The trench collapsed and buried everyone inside! No one knew that the soldiers in the trench had survived. In fact, by some miracle they weren't even hurt. They had enough air and plenty of food and water. When rescuers dug them out six days later, Tom and the others were as good as new. But in the meantime, Tom's  superiors had reported him dead, and the news travelled all the way back to Canada.

Tom's wife heard about his "death," but she didn't hear that he had been rescued. So when Tom arrived home after the war, he learned that his "widow" had married someone else! That was certainly a strange situation. Lauretta was glad to hear that he was still alive, but she didn't want to leave her new husband.

Is this part of Tom's story true? Some people say yes. Some say no. In any case, Lauretta and Tom parted.

Later Tom married a Cayuga woman named Martha Silversmith, and they had four children together. To support his family, Tom got a job with the City of Toronto, sweeping the streets and collecting garbage.

Are you shocked? Do you think the world-class athlete and war hero deserved a better job? Tom said he liked being outdoors and that his years in that job were good ones. In those days, and especially during the Great Depression when many thousands of people were out of work, Tom's permanent job with the city allowed his family to live comfortably in Toronto. And he kept in touch with the racing world, too. In his spare time he became an official for the Around the Bay Race, often donating a prize for it.

After Tom retired, he and Martha moved back here to the Six Nations Reserve, where they lived until he died of pneumonia in 1949. He was sixty-one years old.

Tom had lived according to Onondaga traditions and was given an Onondaga funeral. The chief said that his "athletic prowess was only surpassed by his qualities as a gentleman. He was liked by everyone."

Tom Longboat may have been liked by everyone, but somehow I feel we are not well liked at the moment. Why are people shouting at us and waving that checkered flag?

Oh, dear! This isn't a scenic side road. It's the Ohsweken Speedway, and we just crossed the finish line! Our big black taxi came in sixth. That's a pretty good finish, but let's not stop to take a bow. Instead, let's make a speedy exit. To finish our tour, I'll drive past the school where the Tom Longboat Run is held every year on Aboriginal Solidarity Day. You might like to take a picture of it to include in your assignment.

As you can see, Tom is still remembered and honoured — not just here, but in all of Canada. *Maclean's* magazine voted him the #1 Canadian Sports Figure of the Twentieth Century, and several important races and awards are named after him. Canada Post even made a stamp to honour him. Every year a running club called the Longboat Roadrunners hosts a run on Toronto Island. Perhaps you'd like to enter it yourself sometime. If you train hard and run as fast as you can, maybe you'll cross the finish line **waaaaay ahead** of the other runners.

But first, please help me find my briefcase!

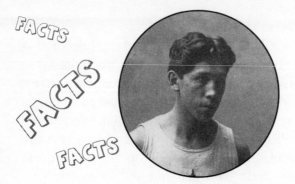

Just the Plain Facts about Tom Longboat

July 4, 1887
Tom Longboat was born at Ohsweken (Six Nations Reserve) near Brantford, Ontario. His Onondaga name was Cogwagee, which means "Everything."

1905 He won second place in the 8-kilometre Victoria Day race in a nearby town.

1906 During the Victoria Day race, not one other runner passed him. He won by more than 400 metres.

October 18, 1906
Coached by Bill Davis, another Six Nations runner, he entered the Around the Bay Race in Hamilton, Ontario. He won the 32-kilometre race by three whole minutes, with a time of 1 hour, 49 minutes and 25 seconds.

1906–1908
For three years in a row, he won a famous Toronto race called the Ward Marathon.

April 19, 1907
He beat 104 other runners to win the Boston Marathon with a time of 2 hours, 24 minutes and 24 seconds. It was the fastest time ever recorded for a marathon.

1908 During the Olympic Games in London, England, Tom and another runner collapsed.

November 1908
He gave up his amateur status and became a professional runner.

December 15, 1908
He won a marathon at Madison Square Garden in New York City.

December 28, 1908
He married a Kanien'kehaka (Mohawk) woman named Lauretta Maracle. Their wedding reception was held at Massey Hall in Toronto.

1911 After some disagreements with his managers, he bought up his contract and handled his own training and business arrangements.

February 1916
During World War I, he enlisted in the army. He served as a dispatch runner in France. He was wounded twice. In 1918 his wife remarried.

1919 He returned to Canada and married a Cayuga woman named Martha Silversmith.

1926 He was hired into a permanent job with the streets department of the City of Toronto, sweeping streets and collecting garbage.

January 9, 1949
He died of pneumonia at Ohsweken.

1985 A plaque honouring Tom's career was unveiled at the Six Nations Sports Centre.

1999 He was voted the #1 Canadian Sports Figure of the Twentieth Century by *Maclean's* magazine.

WiLLiAM LYON MACKENZiE KiNG: TOP SECRET

What excellent sleuths you are! Even though we haven't found my briefcase yet, you've been incredibly smart and helpful. And you've worked extremely hard on the notes for your assignments. Now I have another mission for you. Please put on your very cool sunglasses and open the envelope marked *TOP SECRET*.

TOP SECRET MISSION

Rescue the reputation of Prime Minister William Lyon Mackenzie King (Rex). Learn what to say when silly adults make jokes about him.

P.S. If you opened this TOP SECRET envelope by mistake, please destroy this message without reading it.

P.P.S. If you did read it by accident, please don't tell anyone about the mission.

P.P.P.S. If you did accidentally tell someone, call them back and tell them not to tell anyone else.

P.P.P.P.S. If they did already tell someone else, tell them to call the other person back and tell them not to tell anyone because this message is supposed to be 100% TOP SECRET . . . This means you!

Why do we need to rescue Rex? Well, when this famous prime minister died in 1950 and people peeked into the diary he'd been keeping for fifty-seven years, they were so surprised that they started to laugh, and they haven't stopped laughing yet.

As if that's not bad enough, people sometimes get him mixed up with his grandfather, William Lyon Mackenzie, who led a famous rebellion in 1837. To keep things straight, let's call our subject by his nickname: Rex. (In Latin, *Rex* means "king." Get it?)

Now, if you tell your favourite adult that you're learning about William Lyon Mackenzie King, the adult is almost sure to make a wisecrack about his dead mother. Why? Well, Rex thought his mother was the sweetest, most beautiful woman in the world, and he struggled to make her proud. He went to church often. He studied hard. And when he got a job, he

AND WHAT DID YOU DO TODAY, MOTHER, JUST HANG AROUND?

sent money home to her. He was so obedient that when his mother told him not to marry a certain woman, he didn't. After his mother died, he missed her very much and talked to her often. (That's the part that makes adults giggle.)

But Rex served three terms as prime minister, for a total of 21 years, 5 months and 1 day. That's longer than any other prime minister in Canadian history. *So what* if he liked to go home after a hard day and talk to a painting of his mother?

What can *you* do to set the record straight? While the adults are busy giggling, you can spring a few facts on them. For example, you can mention that Rex did a lot to promote national unity. Please open the envelope marked *Lesson One*.

LESSON ONE:
How Rex Promoted National Unity

1. CONSCRIPTION
During World War I, when English Canadians wanted to force soldiers to serve in the war and French Canadians didn't, Rex was the only English-speaking member of his party to side with the prime minister. The French Canadians loved him for it and didn't forget it. When election time came, many of them voted for Rex.

2. GOOD ADVISERS
Rex chose wonderful French-Canadian advisers and gave them lots of freedom to make decisions. He had a talent for hiring good people and listening to their advice, especially on subjects that threatened to split the country.

3. BILINGUALISM
Rex promoted the French language, even though he didn't speak it. For example, he made sure Canadian money was printed in both French and English. (And now his picture is on the $50 bill! His mother would have been so proud!)

Here we are at Kingsmere, Rex's estate in the Gatineau Hills, near Ottawa. Let's take our picnic basket up the path through the trees.

It took Rex most of his life to create this place. He bought the first little piece of land back in 1901 and built a cottage on it. Over twenty-five years, the estate grew and grew. He collected pieces of demolished houses, banks and public buildings and turned them into a garden sanctuary.

If you hear an adult say, "He built a bunch of ruins, didn't he?" you can smile patiently and tell them about Lesson Two.

LESSON TWO:
How Rex Built an
Independent Canada

1. CHANAK CRISIS of 1922
When Great Britain asked Canada for help in its (rather silly) dispute with Turkey, Rex refused to send troops. He said he didn't think Parliament should spend its time on that sort of thing. In other words, for the first time in history, Canada said no to Great Britain.

2. SIGNING OF HALIBUT TREATY in 1923
Without asking for British consent, Rex sent his Fisheries minister to sign a treaty with the Americans. This had never happened before. For the second time, Canada said no to Great Britain.

3. IMPERIAL CONFERENCES OF 1923 and 1926
At a meeting in England, leaders of other countries in the British Empire tried to convince Rex that Canada shouldn't be totally free to make its own decisions. Again and again Rex disagreed. For the third, fourth, fifth, sixth, seventh time, Canada said no to Great Britain.

What a good job you're doing with these lessons! While I prepare the picnic, please turn up your collars and slink along this wall in a spylike manner. You'll find an envelope hidden in these ruins near the bay window. Please brace yourselves. Our next lesson is very sad.

When an adult says, "Is it true that he talked to dead people?" please sigh as if you've heard this question a million times. Say, "Yes, but his unusual beliefs never affected his public life." Say, "Maybe it was just his way of coping with all those tragedies." If the adult says, "What tragedies?" proceed to Lesson Three.

LESSON THREE:
Rex Survived Many
Personal Tragedies

On December 6, 1901, Rex's best friend and roommate Bert Harper died while trying to save a young woman who had fallen through the ice while skating. The woman died, too.

On April 4, 1915, Rex's sister Bella died. About eighteen months later, his father died.

On December 18, 1917, (the day after Rex's 43rd birthday) his mother died.

On February 17, 1919, his friend and former prime minister, Sir Wilfred Laurier, died. About three years later, Rex's brother, Max, died of tuberculosis.

SPECIAL BONUS SADNESS

Rex never married or had children, even though he really wanted to. But in spite of some close friendships, he was a lonely man.

Even the toughest prime minister would be shaken by a series of sorrows like that! For someone as high-strung as Rex, who had loved and admired his family to an extreme, it was especially painful. And while I would not recommend doing what he did next, I think I can understand it. He became obsessed with the idea that his loved ones were nearby, sending him signals and surrounding him with their presence.

He saw meaningful shapes and patterns in clouds, in his shaving lather, and in his teacup. He watched for coincidences, especially if they happened on birthdays or anniversaries. He thought events were extra important if they happened when the hands of the clock came together (for example, at 2:10 or 8:40) or when they formed a straight line (for example, at 3:45 or 6:00).

Then somebody introduced him to spiritualism. A fad for that sort of thing was sweeping North America, and many people (most of whom were not prime ministers) were con-

sulting Ouija boards, holding seances and making tables rap.
(No, I don't mean rap music, although that would certainly
have made for some lively evenings, wouldn't it?)

Rex believed table-rapping was a way to communicate
with his dead loved ones, and he became convinced that he
was receiving messages from his parents, his dead siblings,
Sir Wilfred Laurier, Bert Harper, and even famous people he'd
never met, like Sir Frederick Banting and Leonardo da Vinci.

But even though he believed in these messages from "the
great beyond," he never used the sessions to guide him in

his duties or to decide how to act. He used them to confirm decisions he had already made and to reassure himself that his family wasn't far away. And during World War II, he spent less time on spiritualism and directed most of his energy toward his work.

Some people slam shut any book that mentions spiritualism. And other people totally believe in it, as Rex did. Others — including some historians — believe that Rex was hearing what he wanted to hear, confirming his own hunches and comforting himself for the terrible losses he'd suffered. Even so, lots of people still laugh at him for this.

However, his spiritualism wasn't the only thing that made people criticize Rex's government. Some people disliked his chilly personality. Others said he had bad breath. He has been faulted for his long, boring speeches and his slow decision-making. Criticism of his government's immigration policies has been especially serious.

During World War II, Canada had a very poor record of helping Jewish people and other immigrants. For example, in 1939 Canada was one of several countries that turned away a shipload of Jewish refugees fleeing from the Holocaust. The ship was forced to return to Europe, where many of its passengers ended up being killed by the Nazis. Later in the war, many Italian and Japanese families were sent to Canadian internment camps. By the end of the war, only five thousand Jewish refugees had been allowed into Canada. That was only a fraction of the number accepted by other countries.

So while some historians claim that Rex was the best prime minister in Canadian history, others are quick to say "no way." Meanwhile, plenty of ordinary adults only remember the stories about his dead mother, the ruins here at Kingsmere, and his much-loved dogs.

I wonder if I left my briefcase over there near the dogs' graves. While you're searching for it, we can tackle Lesson Four.

LESSON FOUR:
Rex Introduces Federal Social Assistance

Here's what to do if a well-meaning adult asks, "Is it true that he liked dogs better than people?"

1. Ask, "Are you referring to his first dog, which was named Pat?"
2. Ask, "Or his second dog, which was named Pat?"
3. Ask, "Or his third dog, which was named Pat?"
4. Say, "Actually, he had compassion for both dogs and people. Permit me to give a few examples with this chart."

HOW REX CARED FOR BOTH DOGS AND PEOPLE

Caring for Dogs (named Pat)	Caring for People
Pat slept in a basket next to Rex's bed. The last thing Rex did every night was cover him gently with a shawl.	Rex introduced the Old Age Pension Act (1927). British subjects who were at least 70 years old and had lived in Canada for 20 years or more could receive an allowance of up to $20 a month. (In those days, you could buy a lot more with $20 than you can today!)
Once, when Rex was away, he dreamt that Pat was sick. He phoned home in the middle of the night and was very relieved to learn that the dog was fine.	When his friend's son suddenly became ill, Rex dropped everything and drove to the rescue with two doctors.
One Christmas Eve, Rex told Pat the story of the animals in the manger.	Rex introduced the federal Unemployment Insurance Act (1940) to help people who didn't have jobs. Until now, each province or city ran its own program. But from now on, you could get help no matter where in Canada you lived.
When Pat was dying (oh, dear!), Rex held him in his arms, sang hymns to him and gave him messages to carry to his family in "the great beyond."	Rex introduced the Family Allowances Act (1944). Sometimes called a "baby bonus," it helped families to cover the cost of raising children. The average monthly allowance was $5.94 per child.

When Rex won a prestigious British honour called the Order of Merit, he wrote in his diary that Pat deserved the award more than he did.	Rex left his Kingsmere estate to the citizens of Canada as a public park.

SPECIAL BONUS CARING
Rex said, "A policy framed on a basis of hatred can work no good. Cooperation and goodwill is the only basis of government. On this line I shall stand, if I have to stand alone."

Is there no sign of my briefcase? Oh, dear. We must look elsewhere. Before we leave, would you like to practise your new skills? I'll play the part of the well-meaning adult and you can be the bright and articulate young people. Are you ready?

Plumley Norris	Bright Young People
I hear that Mackenzie King was obsessed with his mother.	Yes, but he also did a great deal to promote national unity.
Wasn't he the silly prime minister who built those ruins?	Yes, but at the same time he was also building an independent Canada.
But they say he talked to dead people!	However, his unorthodox beliefs never affected his public life.
And didn't he like dogs better than people?	Actually he had compassion for both dogs and people.

My goodness, how clever you are!

Just the Plain Facts about
William Lyon Mackenzie King

December 17, 1874
William Lyon Mackenzie King was born in Berlin, Ontario (now called Kitchener-Waterloo). His grandfather was William Lyon Mackenzie, who led the Rebellion of 1837 in Upper Canada.

1897 After attending the University of Toronto and the University of Chicago, he graduated with his master's degree in economics.

1900 After studying at Harvard University, he returned to Canada as the deputy minister of labour and the editor of the *Labour Gazette*.

September 1901
He purchased his first plot of land at Kingsmere.

1908 He was elected in the riding of Waterloo North in Ontario.

1909 He was appointed labour minister by Prime Minister Wilfred Laurier.

1911 He lost his seat when Laurier was defeated in the 1911 election.

1914 He became a labour consultant with the Rockefeller Foundation in the United States.

1917 He was the only English-speaking Liberal to stand by Prime Minister Laurier on the issue of conscription. The controversy cost him the 1917 election.

December 18, 1917
His mother died just over a year after his father died.

1918 He went back to work in the United States. When his term with the Rockefeller Foundation ended, he wrote a book about industrial relations called *Industry and Humanity*.

1919 He was elected leader of the Liberal Party after his friend and mentor Sir Wilfred Laurier died in February.

December 29, 1921
The Liberals won the federal election and he began his first term as prime minister.

1922 During the Chanak Crisis, he refused to send Canadian troops to assist Britain in a dispute with Turkey.

1923 During the Imperial Conferences in London in 1923 and 1926, he insisted that Canada must be free to act independently of Great Britain. This paved the way for the British Empire to became a commonwealth of independent countries.

1924 He received an Irish Terrier named Pat as a gift from his friends the Pattesons.

1925 He was introduced to spiritualism and began to consult mediums, attend seances and participate in table-rapping sessions.

1927 He introduced the Old Age Pension Act.

June–July 1926

His first term as prime minister ended when the Liberals lost a vote of confidence.

September 25, 1926

He was elected prime minister for the second time.

1930 He lost the election and became Leader of the Opposition. Some people believe this election loss was really an advantage, because he did not have to lead the country through the difficult years of the Great Depression.

October 23, 1935

He began his third term as prime minister.

1939 During World War II, he worked closely with British Prime Minister Winston Churchill and American President Franklin Delano Roosevelt.

1940 He introduced the Unemployment Insurance Act.

1942 He prevented serious conflicts over conscription from splitting the country apart. However, Canada had one of the worst records when it came to helping refugees and other immigrants during the war.

1944 He introduced the Family Allowances Act.

October 1947

He received the Order of Merit from King George VI.

November 15, 1948

He ended his third term in office. His adviser Louis St. Laurent was elected as the next prime minister.

July 22, 1950

He died at Kingsmere and was buried in Mount Pleasant Cemetery in Toronto. After his death much more of his private life became known, especially because of the diaries he had been keeping for fifty-seven years.

EMiLY CARR AND THE ELEPHANT

Oooo! Maybe this field trip was not such a good idea. The woods on Vancouver Island are dark and spooky, especially in the rain. And I thought it would be easy to set up this tent-trailer, but it was like wrestling a giant octopus. I wonder if Emily Carr ever got tangled up in a rope or fell into a creek out here. What a SPLASH I made when I hit the water! Anyway, thank you for helping me. At last we're quite cozy inside the trailer. Will you have some more hot chocolate? When the rain stops, we can search the beach and the forest for my lost briefcase. In the meantime I'll help you with your assignments.

If you think this trailer is small, imagine how it would feel to share this cramped space with a couple of dogs, a monkey and a pet rat named Susie! That's what the famous Canadian painter Emily Carr did. She called her trailer "the Elephant," and it was just big enough to hold her pets, herself and a few belongings. She really knew how to rough it! Outside, a sheet of canvas kept the rain off her cooking fire and easel. Each summer she hired a truck to haul the Elephant to a campsite, where she spent a month or so alone in the wild outdoors, painting and writing and getting away from it all.

Sadly, for most of her life Emily had a lot to get away from!

She was born in Victoria, British Columbia, in 1871 and

grew up in a strict English family. Her four older sisters were ladylike, but Emily was just the opposite — always getting into trouble. She and her brother romped and roughhoused and got into mischief. Emily constantly forgot her manners and tore her clothes and went exploring and generally gave her sisters a big headache.

When she was twelve, her mother died. Two years later, her father died. As if that weren't terrible enough, Emily's sister Dede became the boss of the family, and oh boy, was she a tyrant! Sometimes she whipped Emily, and once she even slapped Emily until she fainted. That was the last straw. Emily got away from it all. She went to art school in San Francisco.

She came home a few years later, but soon she had a new dream about getting away from it all. She wanted to study art in Europe. To earn money for the trip, she decided to teach children's art classes. Emily didn't have a classroom, but that didn't stop her. She took over the family's cow barn. (Talk about getting away from it all.) She turned the loft of the barn into a studio, chopped a hole in the roof to make a skylight (it leaked, but she loved it) and taught the children there. The cow barn was one of the few places where she could get away from her bossy sisters. Then, suddenly, she had another chance to get away — far away! — on a trip that would change her life.

A friend invited Emily to a Nuu-Chah-Nulth village called Ucluelet, up the coast from here on Vancouver Island. It was certainly a change from prim and proper Victoria. The forests and coastline were rugged and wild. If you peek outside this tent-trailer, you will see what I mean. The wilderness scared

Emily and inspired her at the same time. And the totem poles and carvings in the village stirred something deep inside her. As an outsider, she could never fully understand them, but they were so beautiful and powerful that she longed to draw and paint them. She spent the whole summer sketching there.

At first she felt timid. But the local people welcomed her, and by the end of the summer she was wandering in and out of their houses — drawing, drawing, drawing. She couldn't speak the language, so she had to act out whatever she wanted. If you recall my own gestures while sloshing around in the creek, you'll see why Emily's charades were usually accompanied by giggles. The people called her Klee Wyck, which means "Laughing One."

At the end of the summer, she went back to her studio in the cow barn. By teaching lots of classes and saving her money (inside an old shoe!), Emily finally earned enough money to get away from it all. She headed halfway across the world to study art in England. But — as we learned today when our tent poles got tangled in that tree — getting away from it all isn't as easy as it looks. Life in London wore Emily down. She hated the noise and bustle. She worried that her art wasn't good enough, and worked harder and harder to improve it. Her feet began to hurt terribly. Her head ached. She got sick to her stomach. Then, one day, she collapsed!

The doctor said she had anemia. He sent her to a hospital called a sanatorium in the English countryside. Nowadays we know that she needed Vitamin B_{12}: healthy salads and liver for supper! But in those days, doctors didn't know about B_{12}. They thought that the best way to get better was to get away from it all. So Emily spent more than a year in bed at the sanatorium, suffering some scary and painful treatments (yes, even worse than eating liver). She finally got well again and came home to Canada in 1904.

Money was as important as ever, so she moved to Vancouver and gave art lessons to children. During the summers she travelled. First she and her sister Alice went up the west coast to Alaska. They saw huge totem poles, carved from tree trunks, with faces of people and animals on them. Emily adored them. But she was scared. (No, she wasn't scared of the totem poles — although they did fill her with awe.) She was afraid the totem poles would soon be wiped out because more and more white settlers were forcing First Nations people to give up their traditional way of life. She made up her mind to paint pictures of as many of the carvings as she could before they vanished. It was a big project, but she was determined to do it.

Our struggle to put up this tent-trailer in the rain was nothing compared to Emily's summer trips. She survived

scary boat rides, stifling heat, pounding rain, clouds of mosquitoes and other bugs, and long, muddy, rough journeys. Each summer she travelled to a different place — up the West Coast of Vancouver Island, along the mainland and through the islands of Haida Gwaii (the Queen Charlotte Islands). Everywhere she went, she sketched and painted and wrote about her adventures.

After a while Emily started longing for a different kind of adventure. Some artists in France were trying to paint the inner nature of a subject — how it *felt* — not just how it looked on the surface. This was a bit like what the First Nations artists did, and it was what Emily wanted to do, too. Once more, she taught art classes and saved up every spare penny. This time she went away to Paris. But city life made her sick again — literally! It seemed that getting away to big cities was just plain bad for her. So she moved out of Paris and studied with a teacher in the French countryside. She began to paint in a strong, bold style, with great energy and bright colours. Just before she came back to Canada, two of her pictures were included in an important French art exhibit.

Did this mean she was on her way to fame and fortune? I'm afraid not. In France, a few people understood the "new art" and thought Emily's paintings were good. But people in Vancouver were used to pretty, polite, gentle paintings. When they saw Emily's new work, they were shocked. They laughed. They scoffed at and rejected her. Emily's private students left her, and none of the art schools would give her a job. She could no longer make a living.

But she felt *sure* the new art was the best way to show the wildness and bigness of the West Coast. She just couldn't go back to the old kind of painting, with its tame colours and finicky brushstrokes. So she carried on alone. The only people who liked her work were her First Nations friends. Some of them hung her paintings in their houses. Meanwhile, Emily was broke.

But Emily wasn't the only Carr sister with money problems. Their brother, Dick, had died, and the four sisters couldn't afford to keep their family home anymore. They sold it and divided the profits. With her share, Emily built a boarding house. She called it the House of All Sorts.

It was one of those ideas — like putting up a tent-trailer in the rain — that *sounds* easy until you try it. Emily planned to rent out three apartments and live in the fourth. But before long she had to move into the attic and rent out the fourth apartment just to make ends meet. She discovered that being a landlady was incredibly hard work. She spent all her time washing, cooking, shopping and fixing things, and *still* there wasn't enough money. She made rugs and pottery to sell. She bred and sold sheepdogs. But for fifteen years she didn't do any painting. Instead her life was like this:

Clean clean clean clean clean clean clean clean clean clean clean clean clean clean clean . . . Cook cook cook cook cook cook cook cook cook cook cook cook cook cook cook cook . . . Shop shop shop shop shop shop shop shop shop shop shop shop shop shop shop shop . . . Fix fix fix fix fix fix fix fix fix fix fix fix fix fix fix fix fix fix fix fix fix fix fix fix . . . Sigh sigh sigh sigh sigh sigh sigh sigh sigh sigh sigh sigh sigh sigh sigh sigh sigh . . .

Did others praise Emily for all her hard work? No, I'm sorry to say they didn't. Just as they had been shocked at her paintings, they were shocked by her lifestyle. Emily didn't follow the fashions. She wore a plain housedress and a hairnet with a wide headband to keep her hair in place. She didn't marry or raise children. Her family was made up of dogs, birds, a white rat and a much-loved monkey named Woo. When she went shopping, Woo often went with her, riding in an old baby carriage. On the way home, she loaded the carriage with parcels and carried the monkey on her shoulder.

Things might have gone on this way for the rest of Emily's life. But they didn't, because one day a visiting scholar saw some of her paintings. What a surprise — he loved them! He told Emily that an exhibit was going to take place at the National Gallery in Ottawa. Emily was astonished. She didn't even know there *was* a National Gallery! But now its director was asking her to send some paintings, rugs and pottery to Ottawa. He even gave her a train ticket so she could travel east to see the show.

Woohoo! Emily jumped on the train. In Toronto she met some artists who were painting incredible pictures of the Canadian landscape. They were called the Group of Seven. To her amazement they welcomed her and praised her work.

One of them was Lawren Harris. Emily took one look at his paintings and felt her whole world shift. They thrilled her. *This* was the kind of work she wanted to do. She said, "I did not want to copy his work but I wanted . . . to get beyond the surface as he did." But that wasn't all. Imagine how shocked she was to learn that Lawren admired her work, too! His encouragement filled her with new enthusiasm. Emily could hardly wait to get home and start painting again.

Twenty-six of Emily's paintings were shown (and praised) in the National Gallery show. After so many lonely years, the praise and the new friendships filled her with terrific energy. She began painting again, using her bold new style and the new ideas she exchanged with Lawren through the mail. She showed her work and even — ta-dah! — sold a few paintings.

Emily got away from her landlady duties and took another painting trip up the coast. But finally she realized that by painting totem poles she was trying to make art out of some-one else's art. She changed direction and started painting landscapes instead, struggling to express her own feelings about the trees and sky.

At last she enjoyed some real success. Her paintings were shown in North America and Europe. The National Gallery of Canada bought six of them, and the Group of Seven considered her "one of us." Emily the Landlady was changing back into Emily the Artist.

That's when she found the Elephant. Like our own trailer, it wasn't much to look at, but for Emily it became the ultimate way to get away from it all. She fixed it up with sleeping boxes for her pets and storage for her food and art supplies. It was a tight fit! She would spend a few weeks at a time like this:

Sketch sketch sketch sketch sketch sketch sketch sketch sketch sketch sketch . . . Paint paint paint paint paint paint paint paint paint paint paint paint paint paint paint . . . Write write write write write write write write write write write write . . . Cook cook . . . Feed pets . . . Get Woo out of a tree . . . Write write write write . . . Paint paint paint paint . . . Sketch sketch sketch sketch . . .

Emily had spent her whole life longing to get away like this, and she loved every minute of it. During these Elephant years, she painted many of the pictures that would finally make her famous. In fact, she began to sell enough paintings that she finally gave up her landlady duties for good. Yay!

Then, when Emily was sixty-five, she had a severe heart attack. She didn't die, but it made her much weaker than before. She couldn't get away into the woods or paint large pictures anymore. But there were other ways to get away from it all, and Emily found one: she wrote a book.

It was called *Klee Wyck* and it was about her sketching trips along the coast. It was published a few days before Emily's seventieth birthday. A huge tea party was held on her birthday to celebrate her book and her paintings and her life. All her friends came to the party, and many important people sent their good wishes and congratulations.

As if that weren't gratifying enough, Emily's book went on to win a Governor General's Award and became a best-seller. And the book made people aware of Emily's artwork. A few of them even started to like her paintings!

After years of struggling to be accepted, Emily had finally succeeded. In some ways she was ahead of her time. She cared deeply about the environment. She fought against rules that made it hard for women to succeed. She made friends with people of different races. And she was deeply concerned about the rights of First Nations people. In those days all of these things were considered a bit shocking by Emily's oh-so-respectable neighbours.

Late in her life, Emily kept writing and painting in spite of the heart attacks and poor health she suffered. Two more of her books were published, and people continued to buy her paintings.

At the age of seventy-three, she died in a nursing home. But Emily's story didn't end there. A few months later her book *Growing Pains*, which told the story of her life, was published. Three more books followed, all very successful, and all still popular today. But Emily is best known for her paintings, which are among the most famous in Canada. The Vancouver Art Gallery has almost two hundred pieces of her work. Rock star Bryan Adams also has some. And recently one of Emily's paintings was sold for over $1 million!

If Emily the Camper had a million dollars, would she still have gotten away from it all to remote campsites like this one? I think so. Just look at that beautiful sunset! Now that the rain has stopped and you've written such fine notes for your assignment, will you step outside and help me search for my lost briefcase? It's not worth a million dollars, but there's something very special inside. We *must* find it!

*Answer to secret code on page 23:
Bill was an amazing man. He helped to win the war.

Just the Plain Facts about Emily Carr

December 13, 1871
Emily Carr was born in Victoria, British Columbia. Her parents were from England, and her father was a successful grocer. Emily was the youngest of five daughters. A brother was born later and died when he was a young man.

1886 When Emily was twelve, her mother died of tuberculosis.

1888 Her father died, and her elder sister Edith took over the running of the family. She was very strict and proper. Emily rebelled.

1890 She moved to California and studied at the San Francisco School of Art.

1893 After about two years at the art school, she returned home. She painted watercolours and taught painting classes for children.

1898 She spent the summer at Ucluelet on Vancouver Island, painting the forest and the totem poles there. She became friends with some of the Nuu-Chah-Nulth people. They called her Klee Wyck, which means "Laughing One."

1899 She went to England to study art, but became ill and spent more than a year in a sanatorium.

About 1904

She returned home and continued painting and teaching.

1907 She and her sister Alice took a cruise to Alaska. She was inspired by a display of monumental totem poles. Afraid that the totem poles might soon disappear, she vowed to paint pictures of as many as she could. It was an enormous project.

1910 She studied at an art school in Paris and in the French countryside. Inspired by artists like Picasso and Braque, she learned to paint in a bold new style with bright colours.

1911 Two of her paintings were included in an important Paris art show called the Salon d'Automne.

1912 She returned to Vancouver and continued painting in the new style. People rejected her work, and she lost her art students.

1913 Since she could not make a living from her art, she used her inheritance to build a boarding house in Victoria and took in tenants.

1927 A visiting scholar found out about Emily's paintings and arranged for her work to be included in a show of West Coast Native art at the National Gallery of Canada in Ottawa. She attended the opening of the show. During her trip to Ontario, she met Lawren Harris and other members of the Group of Seven. They praised her work and encouraged her to continue.

FACTS FACTS FACTS

About 1930

She moved away from painting First Nations subjects and concentrated on landscape painting instead.

1933 She bought a camping trailer and called it the Elephant. She and her pets lived in the trailer during her painting trips to parks and wilderness areas.

1937 She suffered a heart attack. With less energy for painting, she began to write stories and memoirs.

December 13, 1941

A women's club in Victoria gave a party to celebrate her seventieth birthday and the publication of her book *Klee Wyck*. Emily's friends and local dignitaries attended the party.

1942 On a trip to Mt. Douglas Park, she painted fifteen large sketches in eight days. Then she suffered another heart attack. Her memoir about her childhood, *The Book of Small*, was published.

1944 Sixty of her paintings were exhibited in Montreal, and fifty-seven were sold. Finally people were accepting her artwork. Also, her book about the tenants of her boarding house was published. It was called *The House of All Sorts*.

March 2, 1945

She died in a nursing home in Victoria. Soon after her death, her book *Growing Pains* was published. It told the story of her life.

2000 Her painting *War Canoes* was sold for over $1 million.

LOUIS RIEL PUTS HIS FOOT DOWN

Here's what I've learned about putting your foot down: it's hard to do it just once. The last time I was here, my rowdy students wanted to play soccer instead of doing their assignments, and I had to say no twenty-seven times before they opened their notebooks! It's not easy to put your foot down again and again. Louis Riel knew all about that.

This is where he first put his foot down. Literally! Welcome to Don Smith Park in suburban Winnipeg, Manitoba. Pretend we're not surrounded by houses and sidewalks. Thank you for not playing soccer. Join me beside this rather plain historical marker. In 1869 things were tough for Louis and the others who lived here. The Métis nation had grown out of marriages between European men and First Nations women. But now the newborn Canadian government had decided to buy up this land where Métis people had been living for two hundred years.

When English-speaking surveyors arrived, sent by the Canadian government, they started slicing up the land in the English/Ontario style of squares instead of the traditional French/Métis style of long narrow lots. The Métis were sure that the Canadian government was planning to ignore their laws and take away their property. It was bad enough when some of the surveyors staked out unclaimed land for their own personal use. But it got really bad when they started measuring property that already belonged to Métis people!

That's where Louis came in. His cousin André used to cut his hay right here where we're standing. One day the surveyors walked onto André's field and began using a surveyors' chain, like a measuring tape, to measure his property. Were they going to take away his land? Someone ran for help, and Louis came quickly, bringing a number of Métis men.

They didn't fight. They didn't shout. They just stepped onto the surveyors' chain and stood there quietly, stopping the work. Louis told the surveyors that the Canadian government had no authority over the settlement, and therefore the survey would not be allowed to continue. And that was that. The surveyors took their chains and went away.

That was the first time Louis Riel put his foot down. But it wasn't the last!

First, the colony's current governor was dying. (Uh-oh.) Second, a new governor was coming to take over the settlement, even though Canada didn't own the land yet. (Uh-oh.) And third, the new governor didn't respect the Métis people. (Uh-oh.) Fourth, the new governor had three hundred rifles. (BIG uh-oh.)

What happened next? You guessed it! Louis put his foot down.

Jump into the big black taxi. Let's drive into downtown Winnipeg.

Louis and his friends didn't trust the new governor. They had to act quickly. So they formed a committee and wrote a note.

Oh, did you think they were going to attack? Did you

think there would be guns blazing and people screaming and so on? No. They wrote the new governor a little note:

The National Committee of the Métis of Red River orders William McDougall not to enter the Territory of the North-West without special permission of the above-mentioned committee.

Rough translation:

Keep out!

Just a few days later, two of McDougall's men crossed the border from the United States, read the note, shrugged and kept going. Thirty Métis men put their feet down. They politely escorted the intruders back to the border. Two days later McDougall tried the same thing and got exactly the same treatment. But there was nothing he could do about it. Officially he wouldn't have any authority in the settlement until December 1.

A lot can happen in a month!

Back in the settlement, Louis was getting ready to put his foot down again. He and his friends walked to the corner of Main Street and Broadway. It looked a bit different back then. I'll pull into this gas station so you can see the small stone archway beyond the gas pumps. That used to be the back door of a gigantic fort called Upper Fort Garry. It was the headquarters of the Hudson's Bay Company, which governed a huge chunk of North America.

Louis stepped through that gate and walked up a long driveway to the governor's house. Then he went inside and put his foot down. He told the sick governor that four hundred Métis people were taking charge of the colony.

"Well," said the governor, "if you hadn't done it, someone else probably would have." He was too sick to govern anymore. Once again Louis succeeded without guns or violence. He set up an office and a meeting room and got down to business.

Louis thought that if everyone in the settlement came together and spoke with one voice, the Canadian government would have to listen to their concerns. But everyone on his committee was a French-speaking Métis person. What about the other people in the settlement — especially the English-speaking Métis and the "Canadian" newcomers? Could all of those people really get along? Could he really convince them to work together?

Here's the short answer: Yes.

Here's the long answer: Some people wanted to fight. Some didn't. Some wanted to wait and see. Some didn't. Some of the people spoke French. Some spoke English. Some respected the Métis. Some didn't. Some thought McDougall should be in charge. Some thought the sick governor should be in charge. Some thought Louis should be in charge. Some people — especially Louis — formed committees, changed their minds, wrote lists of demands, changed their minds, held debates, and changed their minds. Some gave speeches. Some lost their tempers. Some lost their notes, and while they were searching for them, other people stood up and gave speeches, and then there would be a question about how to proceed, or an argu-

ment, or a pause while somebody translated something into English or French, and then everyone would go home and come back and do it all over again the next day. It was all very complicated and nerve-racking. But they kept at it. Again and again the people met, in spite of their differences. Bravely and patiently, they talked things over.

Across the border, McDougall waited with his three hundred rifles.

The people finally decided to ask the Canadian government for fourteen things, which Louis wrote down in a list. Eventually, everybody approved the list. Then they appointed three men to take it to Ottawa and deliver it to the prime minister.

Meanwhile, back in Ottawa, the prime minister decided to delay things until he could figure out what to do about Louis. He sent a message to McDougall: *Stay where you are. Don't take over the colony yet.* But McDougall didn't get the message in time. So on a freezing-cold December 1, he crossed the border, proclaimed (to an audience of six people and two dogs) that he was now officially in charge, and hurried back across the border to get warm. Uh-oh.

Who *was* in charge now? Nobody knew! McDougall didn't have permission to take over yet. But the sick governor's term of office had ended on December 1, so *he* wasn't in charge, either. He sent an exasperated message to Louis from his sickbed: *Form a government, for God's sake!* So Louis did. It was called a provisional government, and it would be in charge until the prime minister considered the list the settlers had written.

But McDougall was not pleased about being put on hold. And he had friends in the settlement. Friends who had guns. Friends who had pork.

Pardon? Yes, I said *pork.* A storekeeper named Dr. Schultz barricaded himself inside his store with about fifty friends and enough barrels of bacon, ham and sausages to feed them for the whole winter. They wanted McDougall to be in charge of the colony, so they started planning an attack against Louis and the others in the fort.

It didn't last long. Métis guards soon surrounded the store. Louis sent a message to Dr. Schultz. Roughly translated, it said: *Sir, your group of armed men is too close to our fort for comfort. Will you please surrender your weapons and supplies (and pork) and go home?*

Schultz's answer was quick and vulgar. (Rough translation: *NO!*) So Louis decided to teach him some math:

100 men + 3 cannons + 15 minutes = ?

The men inside the store figured out the correct answer. They surrendered. Louis marched them off to the fort and locked them in cells. Disgusted, McDougall packed up his rifles and went back to Ontario. And that was that. Sort of.

Twelve of Louis' prisoners escaped. Most were quickly rounded up, but an especially tough and loud-mouthed prisoner called Thomas Scott got away. (Uh-oh!) Scott went around town urging everyone to fight to free the prisoners. Several hundred angry Canadians joined him. But when this impromptu army got back to the fort, the prisoners were already free. Louis had let them go. So now a crowd of angry Canadians was camped on his doorstep, all stirred up and ready to fight, but without a clear purpose. (Huge uh-oh!)

A scuffle erupted and two bystanders were killed. Thomas and his friends ended up back in prison. But did they stay there quietly? No way. Thomas shouted at his Métis guards. He insulted them. He swore. He jeered. He spat. The guards wanted to kill him.

Then Louis made the worst mistake of his life. He put Thomas on trial. And when the jury found Scott guilty and sentenced him to death, nobody could convince Louis to pardon him. He had put his foot down and refused to change his mind. So at noon on March 4, right here outside the North Gate, a firing squad shot Thomas Scott twice in the chest and once in the head. He died right here where we're standing. Oooh!

The trouble over Scott's death followed Louis for the rest of his life. When Louis' representatives finally arrived in Ontario with their list, they had to deal with murder charges! But finally the prime minister agreed to meet with them. He approved all of the items on their list except one.

Guess which item caused the trouble:
1. Create a new province called Manitoba.
2. Set aside more than half a million hectares for the Métis people.
3. Make sure that the courts and the government are bilingual.
4. Don't punish any members of the provisional government for anything they've done, like taking over the fort, killing Thomas Scott or seizing a lot of pork.

Hmmm!

The prime minister promised in words, but not in writing, that those who had organized the provisional government would not be punished. But the people of Ontario wouldn't stand for that. The prime minister took back his not-written-down promise of amnesty, which meant he might punish Louis after all. And more trouble was coming.

That summer the Canadian province of Manitoba was born and a new governor was assigned to take over from Louis. But the new governor's troops were rumbling angrily. They intended to make Louis pay for Thomas Scott's death. They were on their way to kill him.

Louis was brave, but he wasn't foolish. This was not a good time to put his foot down. He fled to the United States. Even though he was elected to the Canadian government three times, he was not allowed to come back to Canada. He could not take his seat in the House of Commons. His uncles sneaked him back to Quebec, where Louis suffered a breakdown and spent two years in mental institutions under a

false name. When he was finally released from the hospital, the doctor warned him to "live a quiet life."

It's hard to live a quiet life when you believe (as Louis did) that you're a prophet who will be called away at any moment to lead your people on a sacred mission. He went back to the United States, where he got married, had two children and taught school, but all that time he was waiting for his mission to appear. And guess what? It did.

One day a handful of tired and dusty Métis men arrived. One of them was the Métis leader, Gabriel Dumont. The men had travelled more than 1000 kilometres to fetch Louis. They told him that people in Saskatchewan were standing up to the Canadian government, just as Louis had in Manitoba, but they desperately needed a leader: someone who would put his foot down on their behalf. Would Louis come and help?

Would he? Of *course* he would! It was just what he had been waiting for! He fell on his knees and gave thanks. Then he packed up his family and moved back to Canada.

The North-West Resistance of 1885 was more widespread, more complicated and more bloody than the one in Red River had been. For one thing, the community was not united in its resistance. Many English-speaking settlers and church leaders were against Louis' idea of starting a provisional government like the one that had succeeded in Red River. Some of the Métis people, including Dumont, believed that fighting would be necessary, and when the North West Mounted Police arrived, things did get violent. Louis put his foot down more fiercely than he ever had before — and it ended about as badly as it possibly could. In May 1885 he and Dumont and two hundred of their Métis followers fought a terrible battle in a town called Batoche. They held out for three days, but in the end they were defeated by Canadian troops. Dumont escaped, but Louis gave himself up. He was put on trial for high treason.

Here are some facts about his trial. Please feel free to say uh-oh at any point.
1. It took place in Regina, where only six people were on the jury (not twelve, as in Manitoba).
2. Everyone on the jury was an English-speaking Protestant.

3. Louis wasn't allowed to talk about the reasons behind his actions.
4. Louis put his foot down and refused to say that he was insane, so his lawyers prevented him from speaking at all.
5. Finally, at the end of the trial, he gave a moving speech about how unfairly his people had been treated. His speech left many listeners in tears.
6. After one hour of deliberation, the jury found him guilty as charged.
7. They recommended mercy.
8. But the judge sentenced Louis to death.

He was supposed to be executed on September 18, but the prime minister was swamped with so many petitions asking for mercy that the hanging was delayed three times. Finally, at eight in the morning on November 16, Louis climbed the steps to the scaffold. He was quiet and prayerful. He bent his head into the noose, and . . . well. You know.

Goodness, what a painful story that was! Are you all right? As we get back into the taxi, I'll tell you one last fact about Louis Riel. In 2002 his trial was re-enacted on television using real-life judges and lawyers. Afterward, an Internet poll was taken to decide the verdict. Eighty-seven percent of the voters put their feet down and said he was not guilty. Now, I wonder what Louis would have thought of that?

Just the Plain Facts
about Louis Riel

October 22, 1844

Louis Riel was born in Saint Boniface, Manitoba.
He was the eldest of eleven children.

June 1858

He went to the Collège de Montréal and studied for
the priesthood.

1864 He received news that his father had died suddenly.
Louis left the college without completing his studies.

1867–1868

He travelled west through the United States and
eventually returned home to Manitoba.

August 1869

Surveyors from Ontario began measuring the Métis'
land, and the Métis believed they were going to lose
their land rights. Louis spoke out against the survey.

Autumn 1869

The Hudson's Bay Company's governor in charge of
the settlement was William Mactavish. He was dying.

The Canadian government appointed William
McDougall to replace him.

October 11, 1869
Louis led sixteen Métis in an act of defiance, standing
on the measuring chain to prevent the surveyors
from doing their work.

October 16, 1869
He and others formed the Comité national des Métis
de la Rivière Rouge (the National Committee of Métis
of the Red River).

October 21, 1869
The committee sent a note to William McDougall
warning him not to enter the area without
permission.

November 2, 1869
McDougall tried to enter in spite of the warning, but
a group of Métis escorted him back to the border. On
the same day, 400 Métis, led by Louis, took over
Upper Fort Garry.

December 1869–January 1870
He and the committee drafted a List of Rights. The
list included fourteen items for which they wanted
guarantees from the Canadian government. When
the English-speaking districts saw the list, they
agreed to participate in making a provisional
government.

February 10, 1870
The formation of the provisional government was
unanimously approved. Louis was its president.

February 17, 1870
Forty-eight prisoners, including Thomas Scott, were
captured and held in cells at the fort after planning
an armed attack on the provisional government.

March 4, 1870

After defying his captors and repeatedly causing trouble, Thomas Scott was tried and found guilty in a court martial. He was sentenced to death and executed by a firing squad.

April 26, 1870

The List of Rights was received in Ottawa. The Canadian government agreed to all items and verbally agreed to a general amnesty for members of the provisional government.

May 12, 1870

After the List of Rights (which had been incorporated into the Manitoba Act) was passed by the Canadian government, the Province of Manitoba was created.

August 24, 1870

The new governor's troops threatened revenge on Louis for the death of Thomas Scott. When Louis learned of this, he fled to the United States.

November 1873

He was elected to the Canadian House of Commons but could not take his seat because of the danger that he would be arrested or assassinated.

February 1875

He was banished from Canada for five years. He began to experience religious visions and serious emotional illness including depression and uncontrollable shouting and crying.

1876–1878

He was treated in a Montreal hospital and asylum under a false name.

1881 He moved to Montana, married a Métis woman and became a teacher. He believed himself to be a prophet and a saviour of his people.

June 4, 1884

Four Métis men (including a famous leader named Gabriel Dumont) asked him to help defend land claims in the North-West.

July 1884

He returned to Canada with his family to help defend land claims in the part of Canada we now call Saskatchewan. He preferred to fight using petitions, negotiations and legal means, but the other resistance leaders, including Gabriel Dumont, preferred military options.

December 16, 1884

A petition similar to his earlier List of Rights was sent to the Canadian government, which promised to study the matter.

March 1885

Frustrated with government delays, Métis and First Nations leaders rose up in rebellion at Duck Lake, Frog Lake and Fish Creek. Troops were sent from Ottawa to stop them.

May 1885

At Batoche, about 200 Métis and First Nations people fought against a force of 800 soldiers for three days. On the fourth day, they ran out of ammunition and were defeated. Louis turned himself in to the authorities.

July 6, 1885

He was taken to Regina and charged with high treason.

July 20 – August 1, 1885

He was tried in front of a six-member jury of English-speaking Protestants, who found him guilty. He was sentenced to death.

November 16, 1885

After three delays caused by controversy over his death sentence, he was hanged in Regina.

December 12, 1885

His funeral was held at Saint Boniface Cathedral and he was buried on the grounds.

October 2002

After a televised "re-trial" of his case by contemporary lawyers, eighty-seven percent of voters in an Internet poll found Louis Riel not guilty.

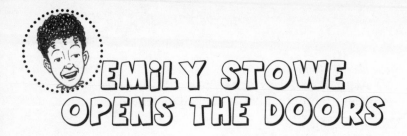

EMILY STOWE OPENS THE DOORS

As usual, people and cars in downtown Toronto are going every which way. I'll stop for a moment in front of 111 Church Street and give you a little background for your assignment. Please lock your doors and open your notebooks. Once upon a time, this neighbourhood was quite elegant. Instead of pawnshops and tattoo parlours, a tall house stood here. A plaque beside its door said:

> **Emily Stowe, MD – Physician**
> **John Stowe, LDS – Dentist**

Nowadays you wouldn't stop twice to look at a sign like that. But in 1891 people would have stopped and stared. A *woman* doctor?

Yes. Emily Stowe was the first female doctor in Canada. She opened a door for all of the female doctors who came after her. And when she wasn't busy with patients, she was trying to open another kind of door. She was giving speeches, or writing letters, petitions and newspaper editorials. In those days people had some awfully strange ideas about women, and she was trying to make them see sense.

What kind of strange ideas? I'll give you some examples, but please try not to shout "Are you kidding?" or "NO WAY!" while I'm talking. Ready?

Strange Idea #1:

Women aren't as smart as men . . .

Please stop screaming. I'm afraid the list gets even worse.

Strange Idea #1, continued:

. . . so if women were allowed to vote in elections, they would make silly choices.

Strange Idea #2:

Women don't need to vote because they can just persuade their husbands to choose the "right" candidate.

Strange Idea #3:

If a woman is allowed to vote, she might choose a different candidate from her husband, and then they might argue about it, and then the whole family might crack up under the strain.

Strange Idea #4:

Even if women were allowed to vote, they wouldn't do it, so why bother giving them the right?

Please stop hollering and waving your arms around. I can hardly hear myself think!

I hope I didn't leave my briefcase here. I hope nobody pawned it! While we drive to a quieter place a few blocks away, I'll tell you how Emily fought against those outrageous ideas.

She was born in the town of Norwich, back when Ontario was called Upper Canada. She had five younger sisters, and her family practised the Quaker religion. Unlike most people in those days, Quakers believed that women and men were equals in home and at church. Emily grew up believing women were just as strong and capable as men.

When she was fifteen, she went to work as a teacher in a nearby town. Teaching was one of the few jobs available to women in those days, and Emily did it for about seven years. Then she went to teachers' college for more training, graduated with top honours and opened another door: she became the first female school principal in Canada!

A couple of years later, she married a carriage-maker named John Stowe and stayed home to raise her children: Augusta, John and Frank. Then trouble came.

John got tuberculosis. Even with the best treatment, a lot of people died from the disease. The only known treatment was fresh air and lots of rest, so John went away to the country to try to recover. And Emily went back to work as a teacher.

Teaching was fine, but Emily had another dream — one that would have seemed outrageous in those days. She wanted to be a doctor. But doctors studied at university, and that door was firmly closed to her: no Canadian university had ever accepted a female student.

Emily sent her application anyway.

The president of the University of Toronto was not pleased. Like most people in those days, he believed that medicine was not a suitable profession for women. He met with Emily just long enough to say, "The doors of the University are not open to women and I trust they never will be."

"Then," said Emily, "I will make it the business of my life to see that they *will* be opened." History does not record whether she crossed her eyes and stuck out her tongue at him. She probably *felt* like it.

Since Emily couldn't get into a Canadian university, she

went to a place where the doors were already open: the New York Medical College for Women.

The college had been started by a woman named Clemence Sophia Lozier, who was fighting to open important doors of her own. Clemence wanted women to be allowed to vote. The right to vote was called suffrage and people who fought for it were called suffragists. She introduced Emily to two famous American door-openers (I mean suffragists), Elizabeth Cady Stanton and Susan B. Anthony. They inspired Emily to keep fighting for women's rights, and two years later, when Emily moved back to Toronto, she was both a doctor and a suffragist, and she was ready to open some really big doors. Look out, Toronto!

Emily advertised her new medical practice in the newspaper and soon had lots of patients, many of them women and children. She treated most of them in their homes, and kept very busy travelling back and forth to her office on Church Street.

Before you start cheering "Yay, Emily!" and "You GO, girl!" and "Success at last!" please brace yourselves. After everything Emily had gone through to get her medical degree, she still wasn't allowed to be a doctor in Canada. A new law had just been passed: every doctor in Ontario was required to attend one semester of lectures at a Canadian university and pass a special exam to get a licence. But — as we already know — Emily was not allowed into the university.

Good grief.

Once again she applied for permission to take classes. Once again the university president said no. He boomed,

"Never in my day, Madam." *Bang!* The door slammed shut. That was the end of *that* interview.

Since Emily couldn't get a licence, she kept practising medicine without it. She wasn't the only one. At that time more than a quarter of the doctors in Ontario were practising without a licence.

If there were a degree called D.N.G.U. (Doctor of Never Giving Up), Emily would have earned it. She really wanted to learn. And she really wanted those doors to open. She didn't want to be told no just because she was a woman. So she applied again and again to the Toronto School of Medicine. Her new friend and neighbour, Jennie Trout, began to apply as well.

Finally the door creaked open, just a teeny bit. Their applications were accepted, not by the president of the university (Dr. Never-in-my-day-Madam), but by the president of the medical school, who said that Emily and Jennie could attend for a semester, *on one condition*: no matter what happened, they must not complain.

Would you agree to a condition like that? Emily and Jennie did. And believe me, there was plenty to complain about. Some of the students and lecturers tried to make them leave. The men left gross objects and even body parts on the women's chairs. They drew so much graffiti and wrote so many rude comments that the classroom walls had to be painted four times! One lecturer even told a rude story in front of the class. That was going too far. Emily and Jennie didn't complain, but they said loud and clear that if he didn't stop, they would tell his wife.

He stopped.

Finally those brave women succeeded. They finished their semester at medical school. Then Jennie went to the United States for more studies, passed her exam and became Canada's first licensed female doctor. Emily was granted a licence later, in 1880.

Ten years had passed since Emily's husband, John, had gotten tuberculosis. Now he was better. He came back home and became a dentist, treating patients side by side with his wife in their house on Church Street. Their three children, who had grown up without really knowing their father, got acquainted with him again.

Meanwhile, Emily had begun to fight for other rights and to open some other doors. She started a book club for women, but its members talked about a lot more than books! They discussed ways to make life better and fairer for women. They talked about education and jobs and pollution and poverty.

But how could women begin to fix these problems if they had no voice in government? As Emily said, "We should not just watch what is going on politically. It's like trying to learn to swim by watching a frog in a basin. If we want to learn to swim, we must get in the water ourselves. We must be a part of the political life of our country."

Women needed the right to vote. But it didn't feel safe for women to talk about these things in public. That's why they did it behind closed doors — pretending to be a book club. But after a while they stopped pretending, and doors began to open, and things really got exciting. I'll tell you about that in a moment!

Slowly the idea of women's rights was taking hold. Soon unmarried women had some voting rights in city elections. And in 1884 Emily tasted sweet victory. The University of Toronto finally opened its doors to women. History doesn't record whether Emily ever said "I TOLD YOU SO!" to Dr. Never-in-my-day-Madam, but I think we could forgive her for *thinking* it, don't you?

Along with Emily's successes, there were some tragedies. First her husband died. Two years later, while she was speaking at a meeting in Chicago, she slipped and fell from the stage and broke her hip. It took a long time to heal, and Emily couldn't look after her patients. She decided to retire from her career as a doctor.

But she didn't retire from her "Votes for Women!" fight. She was involved with two new Canadian suffrage groups. And she helped to come up with a brilliant idea.

Please climb out of the big black taxi and follow me into this greenhouse. You may chant "Votes for Women!" as you enter. In the late 1800s, suffragists in England and the United States were holding noisy protests. Some disobeyed laws in order to make their point, and some got hurt or arrested. But in Canada suffragists usually took a different approach. They wrote letters, gave talks and met with officials. Emily's group also used a powerful new weapon: the joke.

Come right on into this greenhouse with its heady smell of

leaves and earth. We're in the Palm House at Allan Gardens, where Emily's group put its brilliant idea into action. The Palm House wasn't built yet, but if you close your eyes, you can picture them in another building, called the Horticultural Pavilion, which stood here. It was an elegant place, and on February 18, 1896, a crowd had gathered for a special event. Newspaper reporters hurried around with pencils and notebooks. The smell of plants and flowers was everywhere.

Emily's group had set up a Mock Parliament. They wanted to show how women were treated when they asked for the right to vote. Emily played the part of the Attorney General, and other women

pretended to be Members
of Parliament.

While the
audience watched,
a delegation
of men approached.
They were
volunteers —
mainly relatives
and boyfriends
of the women
in the group.
The men
politely asked
the "legislature"
for the right
to vote.

Emily stood up and said that personally she agreed with the men, but they shouldn't get their hopes up because her colleagues just didn't agree with the idea.

She started to list the reasons men shouldn't be allowed to vote. The suffragists had heard these reasons over and over again. But with the roles reversed, the argument sounded ridiculous. Soon the whole audience was laughing.

Reason #1:

If men were given the right to vote, they would soon want to work in women's professions and wear women's clothing. That would turn society upside down.

Reason #2:

No real man would ask for such an outrageous thing. Therefore the men in the delegation were poor examples of manhood.

Reason #3:

Besides, it was obvious that men's bodies were made for heavy work. That must mean they should stick to physical labour and let the women do the brainy work of running the country.

Reason #4:

Men needed to be protected. There should be a curfew to keep them off the streets after dark (unless their wives went with them!).

The audience giggled. The men went away. When they were out of earshot, the "legislators" sat around talking about them — how odd the men had been and how ugly their clothes and hairstyles looked. These cruel comments had been made about suffragists many times. But when the women repeated them, it made the audience laugh — and it made them think. The Mock Parliament was a huge success. The newspapers wrote all about it, and the suffragists made their point and got some great publicity. And everyone had a good time.

Speaking of success — *what* have you found over there under the *Digitalis purpurea*? OH MY GOODNESS! Is that my briefcase? You clever, wonderful young people. Oh, how can I thank you enough?

Oops. Please return this briefcase to the professor over there, and tell her we're very sorry. It was an honest mistake. And don't worry. We'll keep looking. If anyone can find my briefcase, you can.

Emily died in Toronto the day before her seventy-second birthday. As if missing the cake and ice cream weren't disappointing enough, she didn't live to see those doors open all the way. It wasn't until thirteen years after her death that women in some provinces won the right to vote. Soon after that, in 1917, Canadian women got to vote in federal elections, and the rest of the provinces followed.

But even though Emily died before those final doors opened, she is remembered as a great Canadian suffragist and door-opener. There is a portrait of her in Women's College Hospital in Toronto and a sculpture of her in Toronto City Hall. A women's shelter and a school are named after her.

Best of all, when you grow up, you'll have the right to vote, to study and to work wherever you choose, no matter whether you're a boy or a girl. Thanks to fighters like Emily, that's the law!

FACTS FACTS FACTS FACTS

Just the Plain Facts about Emily Stowe

May 1, 1831
Emily Howard Jennings was born in Norwich, Upper Canada (now Ontario). Her parents were Quakers. She had five younger sisters. A younger brother died when he was a baby.

1846 When she was 15 she became a teacher in a local school.

1854 She graduated with first-class honours from the Normal School for Upper Canada, in Toronto. She was hired as a school principal in Brantford, Ontario, the first female principal in Canada.

November 22, 1856
   She married a carriage-maker named John Stowe.

1857 Her daughter Augusta was born.

1861 Her son John Howard was born.

1863 Her son Frank was born. Soon afterward, John (Sr.) contracted tuberculosis. He went away to Muskoka, Ontario, to recover. Emily supported the family by teaching school.

1865 She decided to become a doctor, but her application to the University of Toronto was rejected because she was a woman.

1865–1867
   She studied for two years at the New York Medical College for Women, in New York City. There she became involved with the suffrage movement and met with the famous suffragists Elizabeth Cady Stanton and Susan B. Anthony. In 1867 she returned to Toronto.

1869 She ran her medical practice from her home on Church Street in Toronto. She was the first female doctor in Canada. However, she couldn't comply with a new law requiring doctors to obtain a licence because women were still not allowed to attend the University of Toronto.

1870 Emily and her friend Jennie Trout attended one semester of lectures at the Toronto School of Medicine.

1873 Her husband returned after ten years in treatment for tuberculosis. He became a dentist.

1877 She started Canada's first suffrage group. It was disguised as a "literary society." The group dealt with issues of poverty, pollution, education and women's rights — especially women's right to vote.

1880 She was finally granted a medical licence by the College of Physicians and Surgeons.

1891 Her husband died.

1893 At a women's meeting during the Chicago World's Fair, she fell from the speakers' platform and broke her hip. She returned to Canada to recover, and retired from her medical practice. She continued her fight for women's right to vote.

1896 She helped to organize a Mock Parliament in Toronto to publicize the suffragists' point of view.

April 30, 1903
She died in Toronto one day before her seventy-second birthday.

1917 Women won the right to vote in Canadian federal elections.

MARY ANN SHADD SPEAKS OUT

The old courthouse stands on a quiet street in the city of Chatham, Ontario. As you can see, things here are pretty orderly and quiet. But once upon a time, they weren't. At least, that's how the story goes.

One day back in the 1850s, a young black boy was walking near here when some white men rushed up and grabbed him. They planned to drag him back to the United States, where they could earn a nice fat reward for him. The boy didn't have a hat, coat or shoes — he had been running for some time. He was a runaway slave, and the men were slave hunters. When they caught him, he was doomed. Then Mary Ann Shadd Cary showed up.

No, she didn't swirl her superhero cape. She didn't zap the bad guys with laser beams. But she did have a kind of superpower: whenever she saw evil, she spoke out. Loudly! She tore that boy away from the slave hunters, ran to the courthouse and rang the bell so hard that the whole town came running to see what was wrong. An angry crowd showed up and scared the slave hunters away.

Is this a true story? Some people think so. But even if it's not, it tells us something about Mary Ann and how people felt about her. She was fearless, brilliant and deeply committed to helping people — especially those who were suffering because of slavery.

In those days slavery was still allowed in the United States. The Southern states practised it, but in the Northern states, many people were against it. And in Upper Canada it had been against the law since 1793.

People in the Northern states often refused to catch runaway slaves, and that made the Southern slave owners furious. The conflict was tearing the United States apart. In 1850 a harsh law was passed. Anyone who gave food or shelter to a runaway slave could be fined or sent to jail. Officials could be fined $1000 if they failed to arrest a runaway slave. (Even today that's a *lot* of money. Back then it was worth even more!) If a suspected slave was caught, he or she wouldn't even get a trial. As long as someone claimed to be the owner, even without proof, a suspected slave could be punished and sent back into slavery.

Nowadays it's hard to believe that such a law existed. It put all black people in danger. Tens of thousands fled the United States, and most came to Canada. One of them was Mary Ann Shadd.

Mary Ann had never been a slave. She was born into a free black family in the state of Delaware, and her home was a station on what was known as the Underground Railroad. Escaped slaves would hide there during their journey north to freedom, and Mary Ann's family would feed them and keep them safe.

Her father was a shoemaker. He also printed an anti-slavery newspaper. In those days, that was a dangerous thing to do. Publishers of such papers were sometimes tarred and feathered, or even killed. In some states, a black person could be punished with twenty-five lashes of a whip just for reading one.

There were no schools for black children in Delaware, so when Mary Ann was ten, her family moved to Pennsylvania. For six years she went to a school where black children and white children studied together. She grew up to be a teacher and, like her father, she was soon fighting for the rights of black people.

In 1849 she published a twelve-page pamphlet called "Hints to the Colored People of the North," setting out some of her ideas. She encouraged blacks to fight back against slavery instead of waiting for white people to support their cause. She believed independence and self-reliance were the best way for black people to be free.

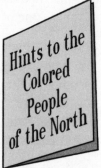

Mary Ann also believed that the best way for anyone to become self-reliant was to get a good education. So she moved to Windsor, Ontario, and opened a school in a falling-down army building. Both black and white students were welcome at the school. But even though the fees were very low, most people couldn't pay. Some people gave wood for the stove, instead. So Mary Ann may have been toasty warm, but she couldn't make ends meet. It seemed that the school would have to close.

Finally — whew! — a missionary group agreed to pay her salary. About twenty-four students began to attend classes regularly. Mary Ann taught children during the day and adults in the evenings. Her youngest student was four years old and her oldest was forty-five! She taught every grade and every subject, including Sunday school.

Mary Ann also continued to speak out about her ideas. She published another pamphlet. This one was called "A Plea for Emigration, or; Notes of Canada West in its Moral, Social and Political Aspect." It urged black people from the United States to come to Canada, and promoted her idea that blacks and whites should study and live together.

Not everyone agreed with her ideas. One of her critics was a man named Henry Bibb. Soon things between them got nasty.

Unlike Mary Ann, Henry had once been a slave. Now he lived in Canada and published a newspaper. He passionately believed that it was better for black people to live apart from white people, in separate settlements. But Mary Ann passionately believed the opposite. As if that argument weren't bitter enough, Henry and Mary Ann also got into complicated arguments about money. Each began to attack the other's character.

The conflict hurt both of them. The missionary group didn't want to be connected with it, and they decided not to support Mary Ann's school anymore. Meanwhile, Henry kept saying bad things about her in his newspaper. Mary Ann wanted to speak out. But *how*? She decided to publish her own newspaper.

A well-respected black man named Samuel Ringgold Ward, who was famous for fighting against slavery, allowed his name to be used on Mary Ann's newspaper. She kept quiet about the fact that he wasn't really the editor. In those days it wasn't considered respectable for a woman to work outside the home, and if readers knew the *Provincial Freeman* was published by a woman, they might not buy it. So

Mary Ann did the work, while Mr. Ward's name gave the newspaper a kind of celebrity and respectability. In this way Mary Ann became the first woman to publish a newspaper in Canada, and the first black woman in North America to edit a weekly paper.

As you can imagine, this new project cost a lot of money. After one issue, Mary Ann took a year off, travelling through Canada and the United States to give speeches and ask for funds. It was hard, exhausting work. People weren't used to hearing a woman speak out in public, and many were uncomfortable with the idea. The money trickled in slowly, but finally she raised enough to publish the *Provincial Freeman* regularly. Its motto was "Self-Reliance is the True Road to Independence."

The first issues were published in Toronto, but soon Mary Ann moved to the smaller town of Chatham, where half the people were black. In Chatham she found a good audience for her paper.

Around this time Mary Ann got married to a black businessman named Thomas Cary. He owned a barbershop and a business that sold ice in the city of Toronto. (In the days before refrigerators, this was pretty important!) Like Mary Ann, he fought against slavery, and he raised money for her newspaper. But after they got married, the *Provincial Freeman* started to come out less often.

In the United States, the struggle between those who wanted slavery and those who hated it was getting worse. In the spring of 1858, a white man named John Brown came to Chatham. John believed in using violence to end the practice of slavery, and he was already famous for two deadly confrontations with slave owners. Now he was planning another attack. He held several meetings with black and white supporters in Chatham, including Mary Ann. But John's raid at a place called Harpers Ferry, Virginia, didn't go well. He planned to steal a hundred thousand guns from an armory and give them to slaves, who would join in a huge fight against the slave owners. But the United States Marines arrested him, and John Brown was hanged. Some people saw him as a martyr who died for a great cause. Many people think his violent raid pushed the United States closer to war.

Several black men had joined in the raid on Harpers Ferry, but only one survived. His name was Osborne Perry Anderson, and he was from Chatham. Mary Ann knew him, and after the raid she helped him write a book about what had happened. It was called *A Voice from Harper's Ferry*.

Soon a terrible war broke out in the United States. It was called the Civil War, but there was nothing civil about it. It was a nightmare. Over thirty-five thousand Canadians, both black and white, joined the Northern states in fighting against the South. But Mary Ann's husband, Thomas, didn't have a chance to join up. In 1860 he got sick and died.

Five months later, Mary Ann gave birth to her second child: a boy. To support herself and her family, she went back to work as a teacher in Chatham. But in the United States, the terrible war dragged on. More than two years later, the US president, Abraham Lincoln, finally said the words that changed everything: ". . . all persons held as slaves . . . are, and henceforward shall be, free." It was the beginning of the end of slavery. The slaves weren't truly free yet. But soon they would be.

Later that year Mary Ann went back to the United States to help with the war effort. She travelled from one state to another, recruiting soldiers for the Northern army. Still the war dragged on. It finally ended about a year and a half later. The Southern states surrendered to the North, and the shattered country began to put itself back together again. But the newly freed slaves faced huge challenges.

Mary Ann wanted to help black people live well in the war's aftermath. But where could she do the most good? Should she stay in Canada?

In the end she decided to move back to the United States. As a teacher and school principal, she could help people who wanted more education. But they also had another urgent need — a need for justice. If Mary Ann became a lawyer, she could help them even more.

This must have seemed like an impossible goal. There were few places for black law students, and even fewer for women. Besides, Mary Ann already had a full-time job as a teacher, and two children to raise. How could she study law as well?

But she did it. She worked as a teacher during the day and went to law school at night. She finished her studies in 1872, but — you knew this would happen, didn't you? — she wasn't allowed to graduate with the rest of her class because she was a woman. Finally, at the age of sixty, she got her degree and became a lawyer. She spent her last years helping black people build new lives for themselves in the United States.

She came back to Canada only once, to speak at a suffragist rally. In 1893 she died of cancer.

Mary Ann is honoured in both Canada and the United States. As we drive through the city of Chatham (still looking for my lost briefcase, of course), you will see more than one historic plaque to honour her. In 1994 she was named a Person of National Historic Significance in Canada. When her name was added to the National Women's Hall of Fame in New York, her achievements were summed up this way: "As an educator, an abolitionist, an editor, an attorney and a feminist, she dedicated her life to improving the quality of life for everyone —
black and
white, male
and female."

Just the Plain Facts about Mary Ann Shadd

October 9, 1823
Mary Ann Camberton Shadd was born a free black in Wilmington, Delaware.

1833 Her family moved to West Chester, Pennsylvania, where she attended a Quaker boarding school.

1839 When she was 16 years old, she became a teacher.

1849 She published a pamphlet called "Hints to the Colored People of the North." It encouraged black people to fight against slavery.

1850 A dangerous law called the Fugitive Slave Act meant escaped slaves and free blacks could be returned to slavery. Many fled to Canada, including Mary Ann.

1851 Mary Ann moved to Windsor, Ontario. She started a school that accepted both black and white students.

1852 She published a pamphlet called "A Plea for Emigration." It urged American blacks to come to Canada.

1853 She began publishing a weekly newspaper called the *Provincial Freeman*. It reported news and opinions for black people in Canada.

January 3, 1856
She married a black businessman named Thomas Cary.

August 7, 1857
She gave birth to a daughter, Sarah Elizabeth.

November 29, 1860
Her husband died. Five months later, her son Linton was born.

April 12, 1861
The American Civil War began. Over 35,000 Canadian soldiers, both black and white, helped the Northern states fight against the Southern states.

January 1, 1863
The President of the United States, Abraham Lincoln, announced that American slaves would be set free. This announcement was called the Emancipation Proclamation. Later that year Mary Ann moved back to the United States and helped to recruit soldiers for the Northern army.

1868 When the war ended, she stayed in the United States to help the newly freed slaves adjust to their lives. She worked as a teacher and then as a school principal.

1869 She was the first female law student at Howard University. She graduated, but was not granted her degree because she was a woman.

1883 Finally she received her degree and began a career as a lawyer.

June 5, 1893
    She died in Washington, D.C.

1994 She was recognized as a Person of National Historic Significance in Canada.

DAVID THOMPSON: NEVER GIVE UP!

In our quest to learn about Canadian history — and to make sure you get a great mark on your assignment, *and* to find my lost briefcase — sometimes we must leave the big black taxi and take other (more scary) forms of transportation. So please hang on tight and try not to throw up as this helicopter zigs and zags through the Rocky Mountains in British Columbia.

Today's famous historical place is right there below us. Unfortunately we can't see it! Thanks to the Mica Dam, which was built in 1973, it's underwater now. (I hope my lost briefcase isn't down there with the fishes!) From our helicopter we can look straight down into a beautiful lake surrounded by steep mountains. But once upon a time, the bottom of this lake was home to an explorer named David Thompson. He was caught up in a crazy, impossible race to the sea, and when he camped here, things were not looking so good for him.

How did David Thompson come to be here? Not by helicopter! His journey to this place, which came to be called "Boat Encampment," started long ago and far away — in London, England. His father died soon after David was born in 1770, and his mother couldn't look after him. She sent him away to a charity school, and when he was fourteen he became an apprentice with the Hudson's Bay Company. They sent him to Canada.

As an apprentice, David had to work for the company for seven years. It was a big commitment, but a boy from a charity school didn't have a lot of choices, so David made the most of it. First he was sent to Fort Churchill, on Hudson Bay, and then to a fort called Cumberland House on the prairies. His new boss inspired him — though not by setting a *good* example, but a *bad* one, living such a sad and disgusting life that David vowed never to be like him. From then on David lived a good and righteous life, safe from the dangers of gambling, alcohol and irresponsible living.

Did this mean his life was trouble-free? Sadly, no. The first tragedy came two days before Christmas, when he was eighteen years old. While pulling a sled near a fort called Manchester House, he fell down a bank and broke his right leg. It swelled so badly that it couldn't be properly set, and for months it seemed that David might die. When spring came, his bosses tried to send him to a fort called York Factory, where he could get better care, but the journey was too hard and painful for him, so he ended up at Cumberland House. It took a full year for him to recover, and he limped for the rest of his life.

But good things sometimes happen in the middle of a tragedy. During the long, boring winter when David couldn't leave the fort, an expert surveyor named Philip Turnor taught him the art of surveying (measuring the land so maps could be made) and astronomy (studying stars and planets). David *loved* this. And he was good at it. He spent hours taking measurements and making calculations. He spent so much time working — peering at the sun and read-

ing by candlelight — that he went blind in one eye.

Meanwhile, Philip was planning a surveying trip into the wilderness. For David the expedition would have been a dream come true. He longed to be invited. But because of his injured leg and eye, he was not allowed to go. Two of his young friends were chosen instead. Broken-hearted, David was sent to another fort to finish his studies.

In those days, when a young man finished his apprenticeship, the Hudson's Bay Company usually rewarded him with a new suit of clothes. When his turn came, David asked them for a set of surveying instruments instead. Surprise! They sent him the instruments *and* a new suit. That was a nice pat on the back for him, wasn't it? His bosses encouraged him to keep studying and working on his surveying skills, and he hoped they would soon give him a job as a surveyor.

But he was disappointed again and again. Over the next few years he managed to make a couple of short surveying trips, but most of the time he was kept busy with fur-trading business. He was more like a shopkeeper than an explorer. The Hudson's Bay Company had grown big and cumbersome, weighed down by traditions and paperwork. It was run by bosses in England who had never set foot in North America. Every decision was made slowly and cautiously. At this rate David would be an old man before he got to do any real surveying.

Finally he couldn't stand it anymore. He jumped ship.

Pardon? No, he didn't plunge out of a boat into deep water! Remember, the lake below us didn't exist yet. I mean that he resigned from the Hudson's Bay Company and joined the North West Company, which was a new, young, energetic business that had started to compete in the fur trade. It was based in Montreal, but by July 1797 David was working at its western headquarters on Lake Superior.

At that time, a border was being drawn between the British and American territories in the west. David's bosses were pretty sure that the line would follow the forty-ninth parallel of latitude (and in the end, it did), but there was a problem. The North West Company had built forts and fur-trading posts in that area, but its maps were pretty rough. In fact, nobody was *exactly* sure where the forts were located. Would some of them turn out to be on the wrong side of the border? Somebody brave and tough was needed — somebody with excellent surveying skills, who could travel around the whole area, and work fast, and make a terrific map. Guess who got the job?

Historians still marvel at the speed and accuracy of David's work. Within two years he had mapped the whole region, including all of the North West Company posts and the lakes and rivers. He was ready for a new adventure.

He got one. He got married. This is how he wrote about it in his journal: *The event took place on June 10, 1799 at Lat. 55.26.15 N, Long. 107.46.40 W.* His new wife was a Métis girl named Charlotte Small. She was just fourteen years old, which was young for a bride, even in those days. Luckily they had a long and happy marriage — fifty-eight years! — and thirteen sons and daughters.

Over the next seven years, David worked as a fur trader and went on lots of surveying assignments. He mapped a lot of territory east of the Rocky Mountains. He met many First Nations people there and did some fur-trading business with them. But he was always eager for a bigger mission. Boy, did he ever get one!

Two American explorers named Lewis and Clark had recently found their way through the Rocky Mountains to the Pacific coast. This could mean great things for the fur-trading business, and the North West Company was determined not to be left out of the action. People knew that the Columbia River emptied into the ocean near what is now Portland, Oregon. But where did it start? And was it possible to travel all the way down that river from the mountains to the ocean?

The fur traders certainly hoped so. At that time, before the Panama Canal was built, the only way to reach the mouth of the Columbia River was to sail from the east coast of North America all the way around Cape Horn at the very bottom of South America and back up the Pacific coast. In other words: it was a very long way. It would be like walking from your bedroom to your kitchen by way of your school.

Could the Columbia River be a shortcut? Everyone hoped so. David was sent to find out.

But it wasn't easy. To start with, the Columbia River goes the wrong way. No wonder David was confused! You'd think a mighty river that wanted to reach the Pacific Ocean would just flow south and west until it got there. But the Columbia took a weird detour. First it flowed north. Then, right here near Boat Encampment, it made a U-turn and headed south. The lake below us is really the Columbia River, made fat because of the dam at its southern end. David was the first person to figure out that the northern-flowing river and the southern-flowing one were actually one river — the Columbia. But it took him several trips, and several years, to unlock the mystery.

In the meantime, it became even more important to reach the mouth of the Columbia River quickly. A fur trader from New York planned to sail around Cape Horn and build a fort there. If he succeeded, his company — the Pacific Fur Company — would control trade at the mouth of the river. That could take away business from David's company. David needed to find a land route. Fast.

But there was a problem. These rivers, lakes and mountains were the home of people who had lived here for thousands of years. When the newcomers started grabbing up territory and furs, the First Nations people tried to defend themselves and their way of life. Sometimes they disagreed among themselves, and conflicts broke out between different groups, and between the First Nations people and newcomers like David. So when he tried to cross through the mountains, the Piikani (Peigan) people who lived near Rocky Mountain House said no. They said if he tried it again, they would kill him.

David knew they were serious. He backed off. But instead of going back to a nice safe fort, he decided to look for another route through the mountains. In the middle of winter, with hardly any food or equipment, and no trail, he headed into a scary mountain pass. He said his men "were the most hardy that could be picked out of a hundred brave hardy men," but he pushed them too hard. When they reached the highest point of the Athabasca Pass, David said, "it was to me a most exhilarating sight, but to my uneducated men . . . the scene of desolation before us was dreadful."

It got worse.

The snow was so deep and soft that the sled dogs couldn't

pull their loads. Even after David got rid of every bit of excess luggage, including his tent, the journey was just too hard. Five of his men turned back.

David was forced to spend the winter here, at Boat Encampment. (No, he didn't need scuba equipment. You'll remember that back then this valley was a lot less watery.) Only three of his men stayed with him. They cleared a square metre of snow and built a hut out of cedar. Can you imagine how crowded, cold and uncomfortable they must have been? Compared to that, a helicopter ride is sheer luxury!

In the spring they built a canoe and headed down the river again, stopping to meet and trade with the people at every village they passed. It was a long and scary journey. The river was fast-moving and powerful, and they passed through dangerous and unfamiliar territory. But in the middle of July, success at last! They zoomed down the last part

of the river with the British flag fluttering from the stern of the canoe. Can you imagine how amazed they must have been to see the Pacific Ocean at the mouth of the river? Seals were playing on the rocks, and a couple of fur traders were there to greet them.

Uh-oh. Men from the Pacific Fur Company were already there! They had arrived a few weeks earlier, by ship. They welcomed David and his men politely and spent several days with them. They may have beaten him to the mouth of the river, but David now knew how to get there by land, across the Rocky Mountains, and this was a thrilling new route for David's company. He could hardly wait to get back home and share the news.

He stayed at the mouth of the river for just a week. Then he headed back up the Columbia to Boat Encampment, arriving in September. At last he understood the river's secret — how it flowed north and then south for a long way, then west into the Pacific Ocean. At last he had found a practical route across the continent. And he had surveyed the whole river, from its source to the Pacific Ocean (but not all in one trip).

That spring David crossed the Rocky Mountains for the last time. Then he retired from the fur trade and moved his family east to Upper Canada, which we now call Ontario. He was still a young man, and he lived for many more years, but he never went west again. Instead, he worked as a surveyor and mapmaker. He helped to chart the official boundary between the United States and Canada. And he made a huge map (3 metres by 1.8 metres!) of the northwest. He also wrote a book about his adventures. Some people think the book is his greatest legacy.

One business deal after another went bad for David, but with his usual courage and determination, he never gave up, even late in his life, when he was still struggling to make ends meet. Eventually he and Charlotte moved to Montreal and lived with their daughter's family. In spite of his troubles, David's religious faith and his strong marriage continued for the rest of his life. He was eighty-six years old when he died on February 10, 1857. He is buried in the Mount Royal Cemetery in Montreal.

For a while after David's death, his adventures and accomplishments were forgotten. Then his biography was written, and people rediscovered how amazing he had been. In his lifetime he walked, canoed, rode and sledded through more than 80,000 kilometres of North America. He measured, calculated and mapped a fifth of the continent and wrote seventy-seven volumes of notes and journals.

These days fish swim where the Boat Encampment used to be, and we have to rely on diaries and notes to tell us what it was like. Also, there is no known portrait of David, so we rely on our imaginations to picture him. But as we fly over these steep mountains, we can imagine him climbing, scrambling, wading and limping his way to the ocean. No wonder people call him the world's greatest land geographer!

FACTS
FACTS
FACTS

Just the Plain Facts about David Thompson

April 30, 1770
David Thompson was born in London, England.

About 1772
His father died when he was two. David, his mother and a younger brother were very poor.

About 1777
He was accepted at a charity school in London, England.

May 20, 1784
He became an apprentice with the Hudson's Bay Company and agreed to serve with it for seven years.

About 1784–1785
He was sent to Fort Churchill, on Hudson Bay, as a clerk's assistant. He spent his first year there copying out the manuscripts of the explorer Samuel Hearne, who was also at the fort.

December 23, 1788
He broke his leg in a sled accident and nearly died. It took more than a year for his leg to heal.

1789–1790

While he was recovering, he learned surveying and astronomy from an expert named Philip Turnor. He hoped to do surveying work for the Hudson's Bay Company, but he was disappointed again and again.

May 23, 1797

He left the Hudson's Bay Company and went to work for the North West Company.

June 10, 1799

He married a Métis girl named Charlotte Small. She was the fourteen-year-old daughter of one of his colleagues.

July 1804

He became a partner in the North West Company and spent two years in charge of the fur trade in what is now northern Manitoba.

1806 He began to look for a way to pass through the Rocky Mountains, to meet and trade with the First Nations people on the western side.

1810 The North West Company partners found out that an American company wanted to start a settlement at the mouth of the Columbia River. David was sent to explore the river from its source in the Rocky Mountains, in the hope of competing with the new company.

Winter 1810–1811

After struggling to find a way across the mountains, he spent the winter at Boat Encampment near the spot where the Columbia River turns a big curve and begins to flow south.

April 17, 1811

He headed down the Columbia River in one canoe with three companions.

July 15, 1811

Flying the British flag from the stern of their canoe, they reached the mouth of the Columbia River. The Pacific Fur Company had arrived just a few weeks earlier and built a post called Fort Astoria, near present-day Portland, Oregon.

July 22, 1811

He started back up the Columbia River.

September 6, 1811

They reached Boat Encampment again. He double-checked the course of the river and confirmed his suspicions: the Columbia River does flow north from its source and then south again after making a big U-turn.

1812 He retired to Upper Canada with his wife and family.

1814 He drew an enormous map showing the areas he had explored in the northwestern part of what is now Canada. The map can still be seen at the Ontario Archives in Toronto.

1815–1857

He had financial trouble and suffered some business failures. He and his wife moved to Longueuil (near Montreal) to live with their daughter's family.

February 10, 1857

He died in Longueuil. His grave is in the Mount Royal Cemetery in Montreal.

THANADELTHUR: WALKING AND TALKING

In the cockpit of this bush plane there's a sign that says, *A tip will help the pilot remember where he dropped you off.* I'm almost sure that's a joke. Besides, we won't be dropped off today. We're going to fly over the historic fort at York Factory, Manitoba. As you can see, there are no roads up here, so our big black taxi is parked back at the airfield.

Maybe my briefcase fell out of the plane during my last Historical Excursion™. It will be awfully hard to spot from up here, but please keep looking. And if you see a seal, a moose or an eagle — or even a polar bear or a beluga — snap a photo of it. You could earn bonus marks on your assignment!

Cree people have lived here for thousands of years, and they're still here today. They were here when the French and British ships came and when the newcomers built a fort. The fort was called a factory, but it was not for manufacturing things. It was for doing business — mostly trading furs.

To the west of the Cree, over there toward the setting sun and a little to the right, live the Dene people. One group of Dene are called Chipewyans, and in the early 1700s, the Chipewyans were staying well away from the fort. For one thing, they were at war with the Cree, and the Cree had guns, which had been traded to them by the British. For another thing, the British had hired some Cree warriors to guard their fort. No wonder the Chipewyans weren't knocking at the door!

The man in charge of the fort was James Knight. He wanted the Chipewyans to make peace with the Cree because it would be good for business and it would make everyone in the region safer. But he needed help. He needed someone who could speak the Chipewyan language and understand the ways of the people. He didn't know it, but help was on the way. He was about to get exactly what he was hoping for.

One snowy day, a party of goose hunters came hurrying back to the fort. With them was a teenaged girl, half dead from starvation, who had been through a horrendous experience. When she recovered enough to tell James her story, he listened in amazement.

She had been born in the very last years of the 1600s. Like many Chipewyan girls, she was named after the marten, which is a beautiful creature, a bit like a small fox. No, her name wasn't Martin. Or Martina. It was Thanadelthur, which means "marten shake."

In the spring of 1713, when Thanadelthur was a teenager, her people were attacked by Cree warriors. A few Chipewyan women were kidnapped and taken away as slaves by the Cree. Thanadelthur was one of them.

She wasn't taken just for her beauty. Like other Chipewyan women, she was a strong, skilled worker who knew how to do all the things needed for survival: hunting and fishing, and preparing food and medicine and shelter and heat and clothing. For more than a year, she and another Chipewyan woman were forced to work for their Cree slave owner. Then one day they saw a chance to escape. They took it!

It was already autumn, and they knew they would have to find their own people before winter. They headed for home. But even with their extraordinary strength and survival skills, they began to starve and freeze. If they continued this way, they would die. So they turned back. Instead of searching for their people, they would try to make it to the fort at York Factory.

There it is below us. The fort comes as a bit of a shock

after all those kilometres of trees, tundra and water, doesn't it? Even today it stands out starkly against the land. This particular fort was built many years after Thanadelthur's death. The one she visited was a few kilometres away from here, near the mouth of the river. But over the years, the river chewed away the bank, so the old fort — and even the land it stood on — no longer exists.

Thanadelthur and the other woman had never seen the fort, but in the Cree camp they had heard about it. And they had seen things like guns and kettles that the British had given or traded to the Cree — things that would be incredibly useful for the Chipewyan people.

But the journey to find the fort was exhausting, there was nothing to eat, and the days grew colder and colder. Finally Thanadelthur's friend died. But Thanadelthur kept going, all alone, through the wilderness. Five days later, half starved, she found the tracks of some British men who were on a goose-hunting expedition. She caught up with them, and they took her back to the fort.

When she got there on November 24, 1714, Thanadelthur was half dead. But with some food and rest, she began to recover from her ordeal. She spent that long cold winter at the fort, learning to speak English.

James was impressed with Thanadelthur's quick mind

and strong spirit. She knew all about the Chipewyan people, of course. And she could speak three languages: Chipewyan, Cree and, by the end of winter, English. She was the expert he'd been wishing for. He asked her to go on a special mission: to make peace between her people and the Cree.

Thanadelthur said yes. She was eager to get back to her people and to help them start trading with the British. So James made a feast for his Home Guard Cree, who lived and traded in the area close to the fort. He asked them to join the peace mission, too. He gave Thanadelthur some presents for her people. And he asked her to tell them that the British would build a fort on the Churchill River the next fall. The new fort would be in a very convenient spot for trading — not just for the nomadic Chipewyan people but for the Cree and Inuit people who lived nearby.

In June the peace mission set off. There were one hundred and fifty Cree in the party, along with a British man named William Stuart and — of course — Thanadelthur. Do you think she was nervous about travelling with the Cree warriors? No way! She stood up to them and gave them a piece of her mind. She scolded them for their cowardly way of killing her people. William said she kept the Cree in awe of her.

But soon they all had bigger things to worry about. Winter arrived, and the expedition members began to starve. Some of them got sick. People were freezing. It was impossible to find enough food for a party so large, so the expedition broke into smaller groups, hoping some might survive.

Most of the groups turned back toward the fort. But Thanadelthur, William and about a dozen Cree kept going.

More than once it seemed they would die. One time Thana-delthur and William went eight whole days without food. But Thanadelthur was incredibly strong in both her body and her mind. She inspired the others. When people were ready to give up, she urged them forward. She walked and walked and walked, always searching for clues that might tell her where her family and friends had gone.

Then something terrible happened. Her little group found the frozen bodies of several Chipewyan people who had been murdered by Cree warriors. It was about the worst thing that could have happened, because the Chipewyans were bound to take revenge for those murders. That meant the war would continue, and the peace mission would be doomed. William and the others were sure the Chipewyans would blame them for the killings. They wanted to turn back right away.

But Thanadelthur said no. She refused to give up. The tracks of the Chipewyans who had escaped were still visible in the snow, and she believed she could follow them and find her people. She convinced William and the others to make camp and stay there for ten days. She would go alone to find the Chipewyans and explain the situation. If she didn't return after ten days, the group could leave without her.

Reluctantly, they agreed. Thanadelthur set out alone.

She walked and walked and walked. She followed the tracks to a Chipewyan camp, where an awesome sight greet-ed her. Four hundred Chipewyan warriors had gathered there to plan their revenge against the Cree.

Thanadelthur had found her way back to her people at last! She had so much to tell them. But she had a job to do. She didn't hesitate. She walked right into their camp and

started talking. She spoke her mind, and then some. She told them of her long, hard journey. She gave them the presents from James Knight and told them about York Factory, where they could trade furs for more goods. She told them about the new fort that James was going to build on the Churchill River. Most of all, she asked them to make peace with the Cree.

Not everyone agreed, but Thanadelthur refused to give up. She talked until her throat got sore. She talked for two whole days. Her voice gave out. Finally, on the third day, the others agreed to go back with her to discuss peace with their enemies.

I wish we could have seen what happened next. It must have been spectacular — like something out of a movie. On the tenth day, just as she had promised, Thanadelthur arrived back at the camp where she had left William and the others.

Two Chipewyan warriors were with her. William came out of his tent to welcome them, and Thanadelthur made a signal with her hand. Then the rest of the Chipewyan warriors knew it was safe to come forward, so they did — more than a hundred and fifty of them! What a sight! Later, William said they were fine men, the cleverest he had ever seen.

It was time to talk peace. Thanadelthur sat on a raised stone, like a platform, so everyone could see her. She was so hoarse that she could hardly make herself heard, but she managed to convince the Chipewyans once again that the Cree warriors in her group had not been responsible for the raid where the people were killed. She promised that her group was serious about making peace. Many Chipewyans believed her, and she didn't have much patience with those who still doubted. She scolded some and pressured others until nobody dared to speak out against the peace plan. As William put it, she "forced them to peace."

Then they held a sacred ceremony and smoked the pipe that bound the peace. Afterward, a group of Chipewyans, including Thanadelthur's brother, joined the others for the long journey back to the fort.

Meanwhile, some of the small groups that had turned back were straggling home, weak with starvation. One group told James that some of William's group were too weak to hunt, another was sick, and that William himself was weeping with sadness and fear of starvation. Just imagine how thrilled James must have been when Thanadelthur's group arrived at the fort — not just safe, but having succeeded in their mission. What a triumph!

The Chipewyans stayed at the fort for nearly a year. Than-

adelthur taught them how to prepare the furs they would sell to the British. She was as feisty as ever. When one of her students joked about sneaking bad furs into the shipments, she caught him by the nose, pushed him backward and called him a fool.

James admired Thanadelthur's quick mind, and consulted her on many of his plans. She would think them over and tell him whether or not she thought they would work. He was especially interested in searching for copper and gold, and when she told him that the northwestern people had a yellow metal, he started to think about a new expedition. A yellow metal . . . Guess what he thought *that* was!

He asked Thanadelthur to go — not just to look for gold, but to travel home to her people and explain that there would be a delay in building the new fort, and to promise that it would be built the next year. But Thanadelthur had recently married one of the Chipewyan warriors. James wondered if the marriage would keep her from going on the new expedition.

Definitely not. She'd made up her mind to go. She said if her husband didn't want to join the trip, she would leave him behind. She planned to leave as soon as the warm weather came, and to visit each Chipewyan group in person to deliver the news. This long, hard journey would last about two and a half years.

But life sometimes throws a bad surprise at us. Please brace yourselves.

Thanadelthur got sick. James thought she was suffering from her change in lifestyle and a lack of fresh food. In those days people didn't understand about germs, and the British didn't understand that their bodies carried diseases that could kill the First Nations people. It was probably one of these diseases that made Thanadelthur and several other Chipewyan people so sick that winter.

James wrote in his journal that she had been "dangerously ill" and he had "expected her death every day." He did everything he could to help, but the outcome looked bad.

Thanadelthur was dying, and she knew it. Even though she was terribly sick, she called the young apprentice Richard Norton to her bedside. He was supposed to join her on the expedition and learn the Chipewyan language. She told him not to be afraid. She said her brother and the rest of her people would take good care of him.

James said, "I am so concerned for her death and for fear of the rest so dangerously ill . . . that I am almost ready to break my heart."

Oh, dear. It is so hard to tell you such sad things. Four days later Thanadelthur died. James was stricken with grief. In his journal he wrote about her high spirits and great courage. He said she had "the firmest resolution" of anyone he had ever met.

After her burial, James gave all her belongings to her mother and brother, as Thanadelthur had requested. He also gave some small gifts to her friends "to wipe away their sorrow." Of course he knew — as we do — that grief can't be wiped away so easily. It takes a long time.

But James kept her memory alive by writing in his journal. The Chipewyan people did it through their oral tradition — telling each generation about Thanadelthur, so she would not be forgotten. And in 1999 Thanadelthur was named a Person of National Historic Significance in Canada. Someday soon, a plaque will tell visitors to Churchill, Manitoba, about the young woman who walked and talked until enemies became friends.

FACTS FACTS FACTS FACTS

Just the Plain Facts about Thanadelthur

About 1695–1699

Thanadelthur was born into a Chipewyan (Dene) clan called the Slaves. They lived on the western shore of what we now call Great Slave Lake in the Northwest Territories.

Spring 1713

She was captured during a Cree raid and held as a slave.

Autumn 1714

She and a friend escaped and tried to find their way home. Her friend died from starvation and cold. She found the tracks of some goose hunters who were serving at the fort called York Factory, and followed the tracks to their hunting camp.

November 24, 1714

They took her back to the fort, where she recovered from her ordeal.

June 27, 1715

James Knight, who was in charge of the fort, asked her to join an expedition to make peace between the

160

Cree and the Chipewyan. On June 27 she left with 150 Cree warriors from the fort's Home Guard, along with an Englishman named William Stuart.

Winter 1715–1716

Hunger forced the expedition to break up into smaller groups. Thanadelthur's group discovered the bodies of several Chipewyans who had been killed by Cree warriors. She continued the journey alone, found the Chipewyans and brought them back to make peace with the Cree.

May 7, 1716

Her group arrived back at the fort. James was thrilled to hear of the successful mission. He and Thanadelthur began planning another mission for the spring of 1717.

January 11, 1717

James wrote in his journal that Thanadelthur had been dangerously ill, but he hoped she would soon recover.

February 5, 1717

Thanadelthur died and was buried at the fort. James mourned her and praised her high spirits, determination and great courage.

1999 She was named a Person of National Historic Significance.

RADISSON AND GROSEILLIERS: FLIP AND FLOP

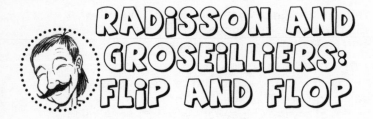

When the first Europeans came to this spot they said, "Hooray! *Three* rivers!" (But they were French, so they said it this way: «Youpi! *Trois*-Rivières!») In those days, boats were the speediest way to travel, and rivers were like highways. So this spot, where the Saint Maurice River enters the St. Lawrence River, was prime real estate. Technically the town should have been called Deux-Rivières. But the St. Maurice splits and flows around some islands at its mouth, where it looks like more than one river. So the name Trois-Rivières has stuck.

Let's park the big black taxi here and walk a couple of blocks into the oldest part of town. Once upon a time, here on the Rue des Ursulines, there lived a man named Médard Chouart des Groseilliers. Let's call him Médard. The "des Groseilliers" part of his name came from his family's land in France. It means "Gooseberry Bushes."

Médard was about twenty-nine years old when he came to live here in 1647. He was newly married and had been living in Huronia with the Jesuits. (If we don't find my briefcase here, I'll tell you more about the Jesuits on our next field trip. Please save a little extra space in your notebooks.) Like most Europeans in those days, Médard was crazy for furs. Why?

Because the Europeans just couldn't get enough of them. They wanted beaver skins, mainly for making hats. To them, furs meant money. So when you see the word *furs*, just think of it this way: **fur$$$**.

Around the time Médard and his new wife were setting up house here in Trois-Rivières, another young wife, named Marguerite, and her teenaged half-brother had come to live in this town, too. The boy's name was Pierre-Esprit Radisson, and he was about to have a scary adventure.

This was a dangerous time in New France (now the province of Quebec). The Haudenosaunee (Five Nations, or Iroquois) people were at war with their neighbours to the northwest. Fur traders from England, France and Holland were caught up in the struggle, too. During one Haudenosaunee raid, Marguerite's husband was killed. During another, Pierre was captured by Kanien'kehaka (Mohawk) warriors and taken away!

They took him to their village in what is now New York State. He wasn't allowed to leave, but his new family treated him kindly. He learned their language and went on hunting trips and other expeditions with them. Once, he tried to escape, but he was caught and dragged back to the village. I'm sorry to tell you that Pierre was punished in the most gruesome way. But his adopted family wouldn't let him be tortured to death. They rescued him and gave him a new name: Oninga. Later, when he travelled with his captors to a Dutch fort, the governor there offered to buy Pierre's freedom. But Pierre said no, and went back to live with his Mohawk family!

Here's the thing about Pierre: he really knew how to change his mind. I like to think of him as "Monsieur Flip-Flop." So when he changed his mind and ran away from his Mohawk family again, he was just being Pierre. This time he made it safely to the fort, and the Dutch traders sent him home (the long way, via Holland!). By the time he got back to Trois-Rivières, in the fall of 1654, he had been away for nearly three years. Just imagine how happy he was to see his half-sister Marguerite again!

Have you ever seen those pink telephone message slips that say "While you were out . . ."? If those slips had been invented back then, some would have been waiting for Pierre:

1. While you were out . . . your half-sister Marguerite got married to Médard Chouart, of the Gooseberry family. Sorry you missed the wedding.
2. While you were out . . . the French reached a peace deal with the Haudenosaunee (Iroquois). You don't have to worry about any more raids here in Trois-Rivières.
3. While you were out . . . the Wendat (Huron) and Ottawa people dropped by. They had to come the long way because of their war with the Haudenosaunee. They're hiding out somewhere west of here. By the way, they have a lot of **fur$$$**.
4. While you were out . . . your new brother-in-law, Médard, went out to try to meet up with them.
5. While you were out . . . you became an uncle! Your new nephew's name is Jean-Baptiste and he's just a few months old. Isn't he *adorable?*

Pierre's nephew had just turned two when Médard came home with a convoy of fifty canoes. He'd travelled west as far as Lake Superior, and he was bringing back a fortune in **fur$$$**, plus some great information:

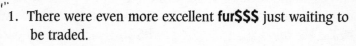

1. There were even more excellent **fur$$$** just waiting to be traded.
2. Apparently there was an enormous bay about a week's canoe trip north of Lake Superior.

Médard had been thrilled to hear about the big bay, which was apparently connected to the Northern Sea . . . just imagine how many furs could be loaded into an ocean-going ship, compared to a canoe! Just imagine how quick and easy it would be to sail them across to Europe! No more packing and unpacking the canoes. No more lugging the furs around rapids and waterfalls along the canoe highway. Médard could hardly wait to check it out.

Pierre got along very well with his new brother-in-law. He and Médard teamed up and started planning the expedition. Then they ran into a snag.

The fur trade in New France was run by some rich people called the Company of One Hundred Associates. If you didn't have a licence from the company, you were not allowed to do any fur trading. But when Pierre and Médard asked for a licence, the governor didn't rush to his photocopier to print one off. (Just kidding.) He said they could have a licence only if:

1. they would take two government officials along on their expedition, and
2. they would give the company half of their **profit$$$**.

Pierre and Médard were furious. For one thing government officials are not famous for their canoeing and survival skills. For another, HALF the **profit$$$** seemed like an outrageous amount. Pierre wrote, "My brother was vexed" and "We made the governor a slight answer." (Rough translation: "#$%%@!")

Did this make the governor change his mind? No. It just made things worse. The governor warned them not to leave without permission. But Pierre and Médard sneaked out of town in the middle of the night. Maybe they thought their trip would be such a huge success that the governor would have to forgive them.

Oops.

After a long and dangerous expedition, Pierre and Médard arrived home like heroes, with sixty canoes and a huge load of **fur$$$**. Everyone cheered when they saw them coming. New France had been struggling to make ends meet, and its economy was failing. Thanks to Pierre and Médard, things would be much better now.

But the governor did not cheer, and he did not forgive them. He arrested them for illegal fur trading, made them pay a fine, took away their **fur$$$** and threw Médard in jail. *That* didn't feel very heroic. When he got out of jail, Médard was still furious. He sailed to France to ask the king for help. But the king refused, so Médard came back to Trois-Rivières. He was mad, but he was still determined to find that big bay, and to get some more **fur$$$**.

He and Pierre set off again. They planned to head for the big bay, but along the way they changed their plans. They ended up in Boston, which was a bustling little city overlooking the Atlantic Ocean. It was a great place to meet other Europeans, and Pierre and Médard made the most of it. In Boston they met someone who knew someone else who was a bigwig in England, and the bigwig knew the king. Maybe the king could help them get money and ships for their expedition.

Off they sailed to England. They were in luck! The king's cousin, Prince Rupert, was running low on money. A fur-trading **bu$ine$$** might be just the thing to make him rich again. And a big bay would be an added **bonu$$$**. Flip! Flop! Pierre and Médard switched sides. Instead of working for France, they would now work for the English. The king and Prince Rupert loaned them a ship for their expedition.

The ship was called the *Eaglet*. Unfortunately it didn't get very far. It nearly sank during a terrible storm and they had to turn back. Pierre ended up in England, where he spent the winter writing his memoirs for the king.

Meanwhile, Médard was aboard a second ship, called the *Nonsuch*, which made it all the way across the ocean and into Hudson Bay. On the shore of James Bay, he and his team built a fort. They met with the local First Nation and started a League of Friendship. Médard spent the winter trading with them. In the spring, more than three hundred First Nations people came to trade at the fort, and when the *Nonsuch* re-

turned to England, it was loaded with **fur$$$**. Even better, Médard had shown how Hudson Bay could be used as a short-cut to the rich fur-trading land in the centre of the continent. No more paddling such enormous distances! Now the traders could sail right up to the doorstep of fur country. Woohoo!

On May 2, 1670, soon after Médard got to England with the great news, a company was formed to start raking in the **fur$$$**. It was called the Hudson's Bay Company, and its owners were going to be rich, rich, rich! The king gave the company trading rights to all the land drained by the rivers that flowed into Hudson Bay. Even the king and his explorers didn't realize how huge that area was. It covered more than 8 million square kilometres and it was fifteen times bigger than Britain. They called it Rupert's Land, in honour of the prince, and Pierre and Médard could hardly wait to get back there. Within a few weeks, they jumped into a couple of ships and sailed back across the ocean.

For the next five years, Pierre and Médard worked hard for the company. They set up forts and outposts in the area and worked as guides, translators, traders and consultants. They travelled back and forth to England, sharing valuable information with the company's owners. But after the first excitement, it became clear that the company was more interested in **profit$$$** than in the two of them. They were never made partners in the company, and they were never richly paid for their work.

They got fed up. Well, who wouldn't? Meanwhile, the French were watching Pierre and Médard go zipping back and forth across the ocean with ships full of **fur$$$**, sharing valuable information with the English. Naturally the French wanted a piece of the action. They asked Pierre and Médard to come back and made them a good offer. Flip! Flop! Bye-bye, Hudson's Bay Company! Pierre and Médard came back to New France feeling nicely sure of themselves and ready to make more **$$$** than ever. They expected to get an easy okay for their next expedition.

But the governor of New France wouldn't support them at all, even though an important official in France had approved of their plan. Now they were really and truly stuck. Thanks to their latest flip-flop, they couldn't go back to England, where their name was mud. And their name was also mud (I mean, *la boue)* in France.

For a few years Pierre gave up and went to work as a sailor. Then a new fur-trading company was formed. It was called the Compagnie du Nord, and it hired him to start a French colony at the mouth of the Nelson River near Hudson Bay.

There was just one problem. The English already had a fort there. As if that weren't bad enough, a third company showed up in the area. What a hullabaloo! Like a bunch of rowdy school kids (not yourselves, of course), each group claimed to have gotten to the mouth of the river first. They argued. They fought. They tried to trick one another. Sadly, there were no teachers to send them to the principal's office.

Pierre and Médard won. They were tough and mean. They knew the land and the First Nations people better than the other Europeans did. They burned some forts and captured some rivals, including the governor of another fort. And in

the process, boy oh boy, did they grab a lot of **fur$$$**. Pierre established a French fort, and his nephew, Jean-Baptiste (Médard's son), was put in charge of it.

Pierre and Médard sailed back to New France, where the governor was not amused. Everybody was still mad at everybody else, official complaints were being made, and on top of everything else, Pierre and Médard refused to pay tax on their **fur$$$**. It was a big ugly administrative nightmare, and the governor wanted no part of it. He shipped them all off to France to settle the mess in court.

Pierre and Médard weren't too worried. They were sure they could count on support from the French official who had sent them on the expedition in the first place. But when they got to France, they found out the official had pulled the ultimate flip-flop. He had died! Luckily Pierre and Médard didn't get thrown in jail, but they didn't get handsomely rewarded, either. And nobody was too eager to hire them after that.

When the court case was over, Médard came back to New France and retired. We don't know much more about his life after that. But Pierre, being younger, flipped (or flopped) one more time. He returned to England and asked the Hudson's Bay Company to give him back his old job! Now *that* took a lot of nerve, didn't it?

The Hudson's Bay Company was not thrilled about the way Pierre had attacked its staff and destroyed its forts. But nobody else had his skill, guts or experience. So they hired him back and gave him a new mission: return to Hudson Bay and take the fort *back* from the French, preferably without killing anyone in the process.

Pierre succeeded. After all, the young person in charge of

the fort was his own nephew, Jean-Baptiste. Pierre convinced him (some people say outwitted or tricked him) to flip-flop to the British side, bringing all his men and all the **fur$$$** with him. Then Pierre took over as chief of the fort for a couple of stormy years. Finally he retired. For the rest of his life, he lived quietly in England with his family and wrote about his adventures.

Médard died in New France, probably around 1696, and Pierre died in England in late June 1710. During their careers the two had flipped and flopped their way into the history books. They showed Europeans how to sail right into the heart of the country where the **fur$$$** could be found. They were the first Europeans to trade with the Cree. And they helped the Hudson's Bay Company to come into being — that huge company that would be so important in European settlement of the northwest.

As we walk back to the taxi, please squint your eyes toward the mighty St. Lawrence River. Can you picture Pierre and Médard down there, heading off in their canoes and coming back again with great big loads of **fur$$$**? In spite of their flipping and flopping, they came back home to Trois-Rivières again and again. Their motto might have been "East or west, home is best."

Just the Plain Facts about Radisson and Groseilliers

1618 Médard Chouart des Groseilliers was born in France.

About 1636
Pierre-Esprit Radisson was born in France.

1645–1646
Médard served at the Jesuit mission in Wendake (Huronia).

1647 Médard returned from the Jesuit mission, married a young widow and lived in Trois-Rivières in New France (now the province of Quebec).

Early 1650s
Médard's wife died.

1652–1653
During a Haudenosaunee (Five Nations, or Iroquois) raid, Pierre was captured and taken away to what is now upstate New York. He was adopted by a Kanien'kehaka (Mohawk) family and lived with them for about two years.

August 1653
  Pierre's half-sister Marguerite married Médard.

1654 Pierre escaped and sailed to Amsterdam, then home to Trois-Rivières.

1654–1656
  Médard went on an expedition to the southwestern shore of Lake Superior. He returned with a valuable load of furs and information about a canoe route to a large bay north of Lake Superior.

1657–1658
  Pierre served with a Jesuit mission in upstate New York.

1659 Disobeying the governor of New France, and without a fur-trading licence, Pierre and Médard went on an expedition to the region around Lake Superior.

1660 When they returned with many valuable furs and information, they were arrested and fined. Their furs were confiscated, and Médard was sent to jail. When he was released, he sailed to France to ask the king to overrule the governor, but he did not succeed.

1662 They went to Boston, where they met some important businessmen. One of these would introduce them to the king of England (Charles II).

1665 The king was interested in their plan to trade furs near Hudson Bay. His cousin, Prince Rupert, agreed to support an expedition, so Pierre and Médard switched sides and began to work for the English.

1668 Pierre sailed in a ship called the *Eaglet* but had to return to England after the ship was damaged in a storm. Médard sailed in the *Nonsuch*, which landed at the southern end of James Bay. His team built Charles Fort (later called Rupert House).

May 2, 1670

A new company called the Hudson's Bay Company was founded after Médard returned to England from this successful mission.

May 31, 1670

They returned to Hudson Bay.

About 1670–1675

They worked for the Hudson's Bay Company and helped to build new forts near James Bay.

1675 Feeling that they weren't well rewarded by the company, they began working for the French again. The governor in New France refused to give them a fur-trading licence.

1677–1679

To make ends meet, Pierre joined the French navy and sailed to Africa and the Caribbean.

1681–1682

Pierre and Médard joined a new fur-trading company called the Compagnie du Nord and helped to start French colonies near Hudson Bay.

1682 They defeated their rivals from England and New England, destroying forts and taking hostages. When they returned home, they refused to pay tax on the furs they had traded. Official complaints were filed against them, and the governor sent them to France to have their case settled. But the French official who had supported them was now dead. Their hopes of being rewarded were dashed.

1684 Médard returned to New France and retired. Pierre switched sides again. He was rehired by the Hudson's Bay Company to take back the fort he had captured for the French. He convinced his nephew — who was in charge of the fort — to give it back to the English.

1685–1687
   Pierre was in charge of trade at Fort Nelson.

1687 Pierre retired to London, England, with his family,
   where he lived quietly and wrote about his
   adventures.

About 1696
   Médard died in New France.

June 1710
   Pierre died in London, England.

JEAN DE BRÉBEUF: DO NOT READ!

Here we are near Midland, Ontario, at a famous histori-cal spot called Sainte-Marie Among the Hurons. This is the gravesite of Father Jean de Brébeuf, who came here in the early 1600s. Every year people from all over the world come here to pray and worship. But I must warn you, Father Jean's story is a scary one. If you have a sensitive stomach, please feel free to wait in the big black taxi!

The rest of you might be thinking, "Well, here lie the bones of Jean de Brébeuf." But please brace yourselves. His bones aren't here. After he died, his bones were dug up and cleaned, wrapped in silk and taken home to Quebec. His skull was put into a silver statue and sent away, too. All that remains here in this plain little grave is . . . oh, dear . . . the rest of him.

Are you all right? I must admit that my stomach feels a bit queasy. But I promised to help you with your assignment, so I must be brave, like Father Jean.

He came to North America from France. As soon as he landed in Quebec he kissed the ground. It had been a terrible journey. He and his two colleagues were Jesuits — religious scholars of the Roman Catholic Church. For them, nothing in the world was more important than their Christian faith. They hoped to convince others to join the Church. Soon Father Jean would travel inland, to live with the Wendat people and try to convert them to his religion. But as we'll see, not everybody welcomed him with glad cries.

The French called the Wendat people Hurons. The land where they lived was called Wendake. (The French called it Huronia.) It's near Georgian Bay on — you guessed it — Lake Huron. With his flair for languages, Father Jean must have known that *hure* was not a very flattering name. It meant "ruffian," "boar's head" or "hillbilly." But the name stuck, and people still use it today.

The Wendat lived in villages and made their living by farming and trading. They were excellent business people and they had become one of the most powerful nations on the continent. There was only one problem. For many years the Wendat had been at war with the Haudenosaunee (also called Iroquois, or Five Nations) who lived not too far south of them. When Father Jean arrived in 1625, the Wendat and the French were being attacked more and more often by the Haudenosaunee. And things were about to get worse. A lot worse.

It was one thing for the Wendat and the French to trade goods like food and furs. But it was another thing to trade *beliefs*. Father Jean and the other Jesuits believed that each human being had one soul and that only human beings had souls. The Wendat believed that each human being had several souls and that even animals and fish and trees and rocks had souls. Can you imagine what happened when those two worlds collided? And the Jesuits were ready to die for their beliefs. Uh-oh.

It's one thing to die for your beliefs. It's another thing to get bitten by a lot of mosquitoes, and that's how the Jesuits' journey began. Father Jean and another priest called Father de Noué joined a group of Wendat who were going to Wendake by canoe. It was a 1200-kilometre journey. Nowadays our big black taxi could cover that distance in less than twenty hours, but back then it took twenty or thirty *days*. The travellers paddled until their arms were numb. They slogged through forests and lugged canoes and packs across dozens of portages.

On that journey the humans may have been half-starved, but huge swarms of mosquitoes and blackflies feasted. Somehow, between paddling and scratching his bites, Father Jean found time to write a journal of this trip. And it's a good thing he did because his arrival was the beginning of the end for the Wendat. His notes are still used by scholars who want to know what life in Wendake was like before everything changed.

Back home in France, Father Jean had suffered a lot of sickness, but in North America he grew tough and healthy. On the other hand, Father de Noué suffered and left — life in Wendake was too hard for him. Father Jean stayed alone there, getting to know the people and learning their language, until politics interrupted.

The English and French were fighting for control of New France, and for a while the English won. Father Jean got sent back to France for three years until the crisis was over. Then he returned to Wendake. This time two other priests went with him. Together they tried to convince Wendat to give up their traditional beliefs and become Christians. They failed — not just once, but over and over again. They tried, but during their first seven years among the Wendat, not one person

converted to Christianity. In the meantime here's what Father Jean did: study, study, study. Here's what else he did: write, write, write.

His biggest job was to write a dictionary of the Wendat language. That project alone took almost nine years of hard work. (Sometimes your school assignments might feel that long . . .) Whenever a new priest arrived in Wendake, Father Jean taught him to speak the language and asked him to collect new words and phrases for the dictionary. Father Jean also translated Christian prayers and hymns into the Wendat language and wrote some new ones. He wrote new words for an old French song and called it "The Huron Carol." People still sing it today. And as if that weren't enough writing, Father Jean also wrote the Jesuits' annual reports (called the *Jesuit Relations*) for the years 1635 and 1636. They were so interesting that Father Jean became a kind of "bestselling author" back home in Europe. Researchers still read the *Relations* today. Imagine being a bestseller for more than four hundred and fifty years!

But Father Jean didn't care about fame and fortune. What he wanted most was to turn the Wendat into Christians. And finally he got his wish. In 1637 a Wendat man named Pierre Tsiouendaentaha accepted Christianity. Two months later another man converted. Then, slowly but surely, more and more Wendat became Christians.

But I'm sorry to say that Father Jean's Happy Time did not last very long. Something terrible had started to happen. The Wendat were getting sick. First an epidemic of smallpox and dysentery swept through their villages. It was followed by a flu epidemic that killed even more people.

People in those days didn't know about germs, but it was clear that First Nations people were dying in places where the Europeans had visited. The more contact they had with the Europeans, the sicker they got. The French couldn't catch the diseases because their bodies had become immune to them over many years — but the germs spread quickly among the Wendat. To make things worse, their enemies, the Haudenosaunee, weren't suffering as badly from the diseases. That's because their European allies (the Dutch) didn't live right among them, so the germs didn't have as much chance to spread. But Father Jean and his colleagues lived right in the villages and longhouses with the Wendat. For the Wendat this was a disaster. The germs spread among them like wildfire.

With good reason, the Wendat tried to get Father Jean and the other priests to leave. First they hinted. Then they threatened. But as we already know, Father Jean was not one to give up easily. Some Wendat people threw rocks at the priests, but Father Jean quietly kept working. He did not intend to leave. Meanwhile, things got worse and worse.

Privately, Father Jean wrote to his superior and confessed that he and the other missionaries might soon be killed.

Here's a little quiz. If you found yourself in a situation like that, would you:
(a) leave?
(b) hide?
(c) throw a big farewell party and invite all your friends, both Wendat and European?

Father Jean chose (c). (Did *you?*) The Wendat were so impressed with his courage that they ended their threats.

But a third epidemic came. This time thousands of Wendat died of smallpox. When Father Jean and his colleagues first arrived, there had been roughly twenty-five thousand people in Wendake. Now more than half of them were dead. By the time the smallpox epidemic was over, only about nine thousand Wendat people were left alive.

Again they tried desperately to get Father Jean and the other missionaries to leave. Some of the Wendat who had converted to Christianity gave up their new faith. People threw stones at the chapel, tore down the Christian crosses, attacked some of the Europeans and threatened them with fire and hatchets. Still, Father Jean and the other priests refused to go away. But they did move to a new part of Wendake. They built a compound of their own, a small religious community surrounded by high walls. They called it Sainte-Marie. Inside were buildings for sleeping, working, praying and caring for sick and injured people. Now the priests could follow their daily routine without interruptions. They could stay out of local politics. And they could grow their own crops. They even had some livestock, including pigs, which

the Wendat compared to "small hairless bears." By 1640 there were twenty-eight men living at Sainte-Marie. It was the first European settlement in Ontario.

That same year almost a hundred Wendat people converted to the Christian religion. For Father Jean and the other priests, things were looking up! But — oh, dear, you guessed it — the good news didn't last long.

Father Jean and a priest named Father Chaumonot travelled to preach to other tribes. But some Wendat secretly went ahead of them, warning the others not to trust the Europeans. By the time Father Jean and Father Chaumonot arrived, the tribes wanted nothing to do with them. Everywhere they went, people rejected and attacked them. They suffered through a terrible winter without converting a single person to their beliefs. Then, when they were finally heading home to Wendake, Father Jean slipped on the ice and broke his collarbone. OW! He was sent back to Quebec to recover.

While he was in Quebec, the travel routes to Wendake became more dangerous than ever. The Haudenosaunee were attacking Wendat and French convoys. Nobody and nothing could get through. Three shipments were lost. Three Jesuits were captured, and one was killed. But supplies were desperately needed in Wendake. Someone had to try again. Guess who accepted the challenge!

Father Jean and two others set out with some soldiers and a whole bunch of supplies. This time they got through. Later the other two priests from the convoy were killed. But Father Jean's work wasn't finished yet.

He arrived back at Sainte-Marie in time to watch the

Wendat nation being destroyed. Because of the epidemics, the Haudenosaunee now greatly outnumbered the Wendat. To make matters worse, the Haudenosaunee had guns, thanks to the Dutch traders who were their allies. Soon there was so much fighting that no supplies or news could get to Wendake from Quebec. The Haudenosaunee made peace with the French, but that wasn't much help to Father Jean and the others living in Wendat country. The Wendat were losing. Badly.

In the fall, 1200 Haudenosaunee warriors left home and hunted all winter. It was part of a brilliant plan to take the Wendat and French by surprise in the spring. Nobody would expect the Haudenosaunee to be in Wendat territory so early in the year. Father Jean and the others were doomed.

First the Haudenosaunee attacked a village called Taen-hatentaron (Saint-Ignace). At dawn, while the people were still asleep, more than a thousand enemy warriors charged into the town. They killed four hundred villagers on the spot and took the rest as prisoners. The attack was such a surprise that only ten Haudenosaunee were killed in the fighting.

Somehow three men managed to escape from the village. Barefoot, they ran through the snow to a nearby village, where Father Jean and another priest, Father Lalemant, were staying. There wasn't much time to prepare before the Haudenosaunee attacked. While a Wendat chief named Étienne Annaotaha and his warriors fought back, Father Jean and Father Lalemant gave first aid to the wounded and prayed with those who were dying.

The Wendat didn't stand a chance. There just weren't enough of them to defend the village. Annaotaha told the priests to run — to get to Sainte-Marie while they still had the chance — but Father Jean and Father Lalemant refused. Annaotaha couldn't budge them, so he gathered up a small group of survivors and led them to safety at Sainte-Marie.

The Haudenosaunee captured the two priests and took them back to Taenhatentaron, where they were tortured to death.

The End.

Pardon? You want details? I'm sorry, but they are far too gory. Please go and write your assignment.

Oh — are you still here? Oh, dear. I don't want to dwell on these historical details. I'm sure they are very bad for you. I'll just summarize them as fast as I can. Sensitive listeners, please skip this part:

1. When they got to the village, Father Jean and Father Lalemant were pelted with rocks, beaten with clubs and — oh, my — tied to wooden posts.

Perhaps you've seen enough movies to know what happened next . . .

2. They were slashed with knives.
3. Father Jean was "baptized" with boiling water.
4. A string of red-hot hatchets was hung around his neck.
5. When Father Jean bore these tortures without groaning, but began to pray out loud, his lips were cut off.

Is it just me, or is everything getting sparkly? I think I'll just sit down for a moment.

Father Jean survived the torture for about four hours. He died on March 16, 1649, at about four o'clock in the afternoon. Father Lalemant died about seven hours later.

Oh, dear. Are you all right?

A few days later, another priest travelled to Taenhatentaron to find the bodies of Father Jean and Father Lalemant. He took them to Sainte-Marie and buried them.

The Wendat nation lasted only a year or two after Father Jean died. The attacks got worse and worse. The priests were afraid that Sainte-Marie would be captured and used as a base for more attacks, so they "set fire to it, and beheld burn before our eyes, in less than one hour, our work of nine or ten years."

It is very hard to tell you these painful things. The destruction of Sainte-Marie is sad enough, but it was nothing compared to the destruction of the Wendat. Most of the survivors took refuge with other nations. Some of them joined the Haudenosaunee. A small group fled west to what we now call Oklahoma, and a larger group settled in a town called Loretteville, near Quebec City. During the hard year after Father Jean's death, about one-third of the Wendat converted to Christianity. When they moved away from Wendake, they shared their new beliefs with other First Nations people, and Christianity began to spread.

And Father Jean was not forgotten. In 1930 Pope Pius XI proclaimed him to be a saint. Father Jean and seven of his companions are known as the Canadian Martyrs — the first officially recognized saints in North America.

Just the Plain Facts about Jean de Brébeuf

March 25, 1593
Jean de Brébeuf was born in Normandy, France.

1617–1619
He studied at a Jesuit college in Rouen, France.

1619–1621
He was a teacher at the college.

1621 He suffered a long illness, but managed to prepare for the priesthood.

1622 He became a priest.

1622–1625
He worked at the college as a steward.

June 1625
He arrived in New France (Quebec).

Winter 1625–1626
He spent the winter with a group of Montagnais people near the colony at Quebec.

1626 He travelled to Wendake (Huronia) by canoe. He and another priest set up a mission near what is now called Georgian Bay. They hoped to convert many Wendat (Huron) people to Christianity. The other priest found life there too hard, and was called back to Quebec. Father Jean continued at the mission by himself.

1629 The colony at Quebec was attacked by the English. Father Jean was called back to Quebec quickly. When the English captured Quebec, he and the other missionaries were sent back to France.

1633 After the colony was given back to the French, Father Jean returned to New France.

1634 Along with two others, he returned to Wendake. He was assigned to start up a new mission. He chose to build it at a village called Ihonatiria (Saint-Joseph Island).

1634 He had little success in converting the Wendat to Christianity. Also, the European newcomers had brought diseases that were causing many deaths among the Wendat.

1636–1639
More diseases broke out. The Jesuits refused to leave. More than half of the Wendat people had died during three epidemics. The survivors turned against the Europeans, and violence broke out.

1639 The Jesuits built a separate community with a high fence around it. It was called Sainte-Marie.

1640–1641
Father Jean and another priest travelled to meet with some tribes north of Lake Erie but weren't able to convert any of the people to Christianity. On the way home, Father Jean broke his collarbone.

1642 He went back to Quebec to recover. Meanwhile, war had broken out between the Wendat and their enemies, the Haudenosaunee (Five Nations, or Iroquois).

1644 Three convoys trying to travel from Quebec to Wendake were destroyed by the Haudenosaunee. Father Jean joined a fourth convoy and managed to get back to Sainte-Marie.

1645 The Haudenosaunee made peace with the French, but their war against the Wendat continued. Some missionaries were killed and their missions were burned.

March 16, 1649
Father Jean and another priest were captured by the Haudenosaunee. They were tortured and killed at the village of Taenhatentaron (Saint-Ignace) in Wendake (now called Midland, Ontario).

1930 Pope Pius XI proclaimed Father Jean and seven of his companions to be saints. The shrine at Sainte-Marie Among the Hurons is visited by religious pilgrims from all over the world.

HENRY HUDSON: FROM BAD TO WORSE

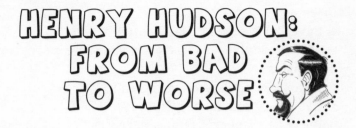

I'm sorry that our search for my lost briefcase has ended in disappointment. But I'm glad I could help you with your assignments along the way. Let's drive back to the garage and finish writing up our notes. If you get chilly, there's a Hudson's Bay blanket on the backseat. Yes it *is* named after the famous explorer Henry Hudson. How clever of you! To be precise it was named after the company that was named after the bay that was named after him. It's a warm and historical blanket, indeed. Please make yourselves cozy while I tell you about Henry. I'm sorry, but it's a grim tale, and it ends with the sad and scary words: **THEY WERE NEVER SEEN AGAIN.**

Brace yourselves.

Henry wasn't searching for a lost briefcase. He was searching for a new route to Asia. The old route had been cut off one hundred and fifty years earlier, when the great city of Constantinople (now called Istanbul) was captured by its enemies. But people in Europe were as hungry as ever for goods from Asia — especially silk, precious metals and spices. Adventurers like Henry thought there *must* be a way to sail across the top of the world from the Atlantic Ocean to the Pacific. The person who found it would be a hero (and also rich beyond his wildest dreams).

In those days, scholars had a nifty theory:
1. Near the North Pole, the summer sun shone all day and all night.
2. Therefore the weather must be warm.
3. Therefore the ice must melt.
4. Therefore all an explorer had to do was find that open water and sail straight across the top of the world to Asia.

Easy-peasey. Right?

Oh brother.

Henry's family was involved with a company called the Merchant Adventurers, and they were looking for this passage to Asia. We think Henry probably worked on their ships when he was a boy. In turn, his teenaged son John served as ship's boy on Henry's voyages. Historians call these The Voyage of 1607, The Voyage of 1608, The Voyage of 1609 and The Voyage of 1610, but I like to call them The Oops Voyage, The Very Scary Voyage, The Mega-Scary Voyage and The Ultra-Scary Voyage With the Sad Ending.

Those voyages would have been difficult for any explorer, but Henry's spicy personality made the everyday dangers even juicier. His crew were guaranteed a wild ride.

As an added bonus, a troublemaker named Robert Juet joined his crew. Robert managed to cause a scene even before the ship left the dock! While Henry and the others were in church, praying for a safe voyage, Robert was having a party in his cabin. When it was time to sail, his friends wouldn't leave — they had to be sent off the ship. But did Robert apologize? No way! He argued with Henry, sulked and showed up late for duty. And that was just the first day! Henry said Robert was "filled with mean tempers." So why did he hire him again and again? Probably a good navigator was worth the trouble.

THE OOPS VOYAGE

In 1607 Henry sailed northeast from England in a ship called the *Hopewell*, in search of a shortcut to Asia.

Here's what he *didn't* find: a shortcut to Asia.

Here's what he *did* find: a lot of whales.

This was good news for Henry's employers. In fact he became known as "the grandfather of the English whaling industry." But he would rather have been called "the grandfather of finding the shortcut to Asia," so in 1608 he went on a new voyage.

THE VERY SCARY VOYAGE

Henry was sent to explore the Russian Arctic, but all he found there was ice and more ice. He turned the ship around. His crew may have thought they were going home, but they got a nasty surprise. Henry sailed right past England and kept going — through storms and heavy seas — and started across the Atlantic Ocean.

Historians don't know exactly what happened out there, but perhaps you can figure it out from the following six clues:

CLUES ➤

1. The ship stopped.
2. Henry signed a document that said something like, *I'm turning the ship around and going back to England. And by the way, nobody on my crew talked me into this. Or threatened me. Or forced me in any way. This is totally my own idea. Honest. (P.S. Did I mention that Robert Juet was aboard?)*
3. The *Hopewell* turned around.
4. It went back to England.
5. Its crew members were not put on trial for mutiny, and nobody was sentenced to death.
6. Whew!

THE MEGA-SCARY VOYAGE

The English ship owners didn't send Henry on another voyage. (Gee, I wonder why.) But Henry didn't quit. He went to work for the Dutch East India Company. His new employers sent him to the Russian Arctic in a tubby little ship called the *Half Moon*. They made him promise not even to *think* about North America. But Henry was Henry — he took one look at the Russian ice and turned the ship around. He sailed straight across the Atlantic to the place where New York City stands today (although he didn't stop to do any sightseeing) and partway up a river that is now called the Hudson. (Guess why.) On that trip Robert and his friends attacked some Penawahpskewi (Penobscot) people, drove them out of their homes and stole everything they could get their hands on.

Robert used the excuse, "If we hadn't done it to them, they would have done it to us." Later someone *would* do it to him. But not yet.

Henry couldn't return to the Dutch East India Company because he had broken his promise so badly. Instead he sailed the *Half Moon* home to England. The English arrested him for sailing under the Dutch flag and told him never to work for a foreign country again.

Here's one bad thing about Henry: He didn't know when to quit.

Here's one good thing about Henry: He didn't know when to quit.

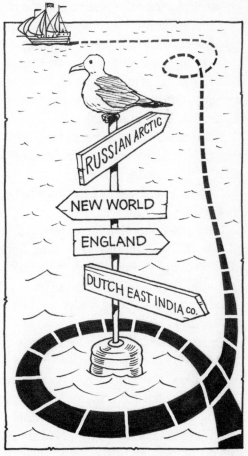

THE ULTRA-SCARY VOYAGE WITH THE SAD ENDING

In 1610 Henry was sent to explore the icy ocean north of North America in a ship called the *Discovery*. His crew included his son John and you-know-who. (Uh-oh.)

They made it all the way to Iceland before trouble broke out. Robert accused Henry of hiring a spy to tattle on the crew. Henry flew into a rage and threatened to put Robert ashore. The crew talked him out of it, and instead Henry did nothing. Too much punishment or too little — both seemed unfair. The crew grumbled.

But that was just the beginning. Then they sailed through a terrible passage called the Furious Overfall. (The name says it all.) Deadly currents pushed the ship this way and that. Chunks and slabs of ice smashed into it. Henry and his crew grew sick with fear.

Good old Robert led the others in a revolt. They demanded that the ship be turned around. Somehow Henry talked his way out of it. He even let them choose whether or not to go home! They chose to keep going, but they no longer trusted Henry to be a strong leader . . . and more trouble was on the horizon.

Does all this talk about ice make you feel very chilly? I'm sure Henry's crew would have liked a nice warm Hudson's Bay blanket. Unfortunately it hadn't been invented yet.

Henry waited more than six weeks to punish Robert for leading the mutiny. During that time, he turned the ship south into what's now called Hudson Bay. (Guess why.) He sailed this way and that, very slowly, through a very scary atmosphere of "indescribable gloom."

Then, all of a sudden, things looked brighter. A couple of crew members went ashore and came back excited. They'd seen grass and lots of water birds. After the indescribable gloom, this must have seemed like a miracle. Henry was sure he had found the secret passage at last. Why, this must be the Pacific Ocean!

Oops.

Henry felt so great that he decided to punish Robert at last. Mutineers were usually hanged, but that wasn't Henry's style. Instead he gave Robert's job to another crew member, apologized for disgracing him and said that if Robert would behave himself, they could just forget about that little mutiny attempt. But this nice-guy behaviour didn't make Henry pop-

ular with the crew. They despised him for being weak and unpredictable. And things got even worse.

He started sailing back and forth across the bay. Nobody is sure why. Some historians think he was looking for the Spice Islands, which were actually on the other side of the world. Others think he was looking for gold. Still others think he might have been discouraged. Or lost!

As if that weren't bad enough, the *Discovery* lost its anchor. Then it crashed into some rocks and had to be repaired. Then winter came.

The ship's carpenter offered to build a shack to shelter the crew, but Henry just scoffed at him. Then, as the weather grew colder and the wood froze as hard as rock and the nails were like icicles, Henry changed his mind. He ordered the carpenter to build the shack. The carpenter was furious. He said no way!

Henry swore at him. And hit him. And threatened to hang him. Then, as always, he apologized. After all that, the carpenter built the shack. But I'm afraid it didn't give much shelter from the fierce winter.

Brrr! Just thinking about it makes me shiver. Is the blanket keeping you warm enough?

A crew member died and was buried in the frozen earth. According to tradition the others got ready to auction off his belongings. The auction money would be given to the dead man's family, and his clothes and blankets would help keep the crew a bit warmer. But when one of Henry's favourite crew members admired the dead man's warm cloak, Henry just handed it over to him as a gift! The others were horrified.

Soon afterward, Henry quarrelled with the man to whom he'd given the cloak. As usual he lost his temper and made a bad situation worse. While the man was out hunting, Henry took back the cloak and gave it to someone else!

Now everybody was mad. Tempers flared. It didn't help that food was growing more and more scarce. To survive, the crew was forced to eat moss and frogs. Yuck!

Henry turned the ship around, but it was too late. Little food was left for the voyage home. Each crew member was given 1 pound of bread and 3 pounds of cheese for the journey — that's less than half a kilogram of bread and just over a kilogram and a half of cheese. It wasn't enough. The crew accused Henry of holding back food. He accused them of doing the same.

To prove it he did a terrible thing — he broke into their sea-chests. He found thirty loaves of bread and took them away, but that wasn't the point. A sailor's sea-chest was the only thing that belonged to him on a crowded ship. It was private and off limits, even to the captain. This time Henry had gone too far.

Three days later the crew fought back. They grabbed Henry and seven others — including Henry's son — and shoved them into the small boat, called a shallop, that was used for travelling from the ship to the shore. The mutineers tossed some clothes and blankets into the shallop, but everyone knew that the prisoners didn't stand a chance. They were doomed.

It was a heart-wrenching scene. Loyal to the last, the ship's carpenter insisted on joining Henry and the others. He climbed into the shallop. Henry shouted a warning to the

mutineers to beware of Robert, but they shouted back that Robert wasn't their leader. Then they slashed the rope and set the shallop adrift.

As the *Discovery* sailed away, the shallop chased her. This was a brave and pathetic ending to a tragic story. The ship slowed down while the mutineers searched for food, warm clothes and blankets. When they looked back, the shallop was beginning to catch up. Some of the crew wanted to let Henry and the others back aboard, but their leaders said no. They hoisted more sails.

Please brace yourselves.

Discovery raced away as if their enemies were hot on their heels. And Henry and the others? **THEY WERE NEVER SEEN AGAIN.**

We don't know what happened to them. Later there were a few vague rumours and reports. One visitor to the area said he saw a shipwrecked English boat. Others said Henry had tried to steal food from some First Nations people there and been killed. But nobody really knows.

We *do* know what happened to the mutineers. Some were killed in an ambush near an Inuit settlement, and others died of starvation, including Robert. Only eight crew members made it back to England alive. Some were put on trial for mutiny and murder, but none was convicted.

In spite of his mistakes — and his hot temper — Henry had travelled for hundred of kilometres through lands where no European had gone before. He kept such good notes that others were soon able to finish mapping Hudson Bay. Within five years, they knew they would not find the Northwest Passage to Asia there. But soon the enormous bay would be at the centre of the fur trade. And thousands of Hudson's Bay blankets would be traded there!

I'm afraid that, like Henry Hudson, my lost briefcase **WILL NEVER BE SEEN AGAIN**. But thank you for joining me in my search. Your sharp eyes and clever ideas have been a great help, and it has been such a comfort to have you along. Now, let's go back to the garage. We'll soon have your assignments polished up and ready to hand in. And I think I have some ice cream in the fridge. Brrrrr!

Just the Plain Facts about Henry Hudson

About 1570

Henry Hudson was born in England. Little is known about his early life.

About 1592

He married a woman named Katherine. They had three sons: Richard, John and Oliver. John served as ship's boy on all four of his father's voyages.

1607 He sailed north to look for a route to Asia. He did not find it, but he sailed farther north than any European had ever gone.

1608 He tried again to find a northern passage to Asia through the Russian Arctic. He failed to find it, but turned around and sailed toward North America instead. When his crew rebelled, he was forced to return home.

1609 He tried again in a Dutch ship called the *Half Moon*. The ship was blocked by ice, and the crew refused to continue. Henry headed back toward North America.

He sailed up the river from present-day New York City toward Albany. When he returned to England, he was ordered not to sail for the Dutch again, or for any other country except England.

1610 He sailed from London, England, in a ship called the *Discovery*, looking once more for the Northwest Passage to Asia. He entered Hudson Bay and sailed back and forth in James Bay, perhaps looking for a route to the Spice Islands.

Winter 1610–1611

He and his crew spent the winter on the shore of James Bay near the present-day Rupert River.

June 12, 1611

The *Discovery* began its voyage home. The crew members were starving. Henry divided the remaining food among them, but they believed he was holding some back.

About June 22, 1611

The crew mutinied, forcing Henry, his son and six others into a boat, along with a loyal crew member who refused to abandon them. The small boat chased after the *Discovery*, but the mutineers raced away. A handful of them made it home to England. Henry and the men in the smaller boat were never seen again.

CONCLUSION: SOMETHING DELICIOUS

Here we are, back at the garage. I'm sorry we didn't find my lost briefcase, but we had some good field trips, didn't we? And I hope you collected all the information you needed for your assignments. Before I help you write your essays, let's have a snack. Spread the Hudson's Bay blanket on the tool bench as a tablecloth while I fetch the ice cream.

EEEEEEEE!

Oh my goodness! *Look!* My lost briefcase is in the *fridge!* What on earth is it doing in there? I'm . . . speechless! I'm overjoyed! I'm *so relieved!*

I'll show you what's inside . . . but *shhh!* Remember that it's top secret — that's why it was packed away in these flat boxes. Of course, during the press conference it will be properly assembled and displayed on a tray with garlands and beautiful lighting. As soon as it's revealed to the world, I'll be famous again. And when the EIICS (Extremely Important Institute of Canadian Studies) sees it, they'll be sure to hire me back.

Don't get me wrong. I love driving the big black taxi, and it has been wonderful to work with clever young people like yourselves. Still, it will feel good to win back the respect of my colleagues.

And now, ta dah! I give you . . . the *Cheese Map!*

Isn't it amazing? I've been working on it for months. It's a map of Canada made entirely out of cheese. As you can see, the northern regions are made of snowy-white cream cheese. The mountains were sculpted from cheddar. The foam on the ocean waves is grated Parmesan, nice and salty. And . . . OH NO!

Somebody has been eating my secret project!

Look! Prince Edward Island is totally gone. There's a huge bite out of Alberta. And all of southern Ontario has been devoured. My map is ruined!

How could this happen?

It took weeks to get the lettering right. (Those squeeze-cheese nozzles are very tricky.) It used to say *True North Strong and Free*, but now it says *True North Strong* and *F*— Oh, dear. I'll just erase that bit with my finger.

I know who did this. It must be that rowdy group of students from my last excursion. I'm so disappointed in them. Luckily, though, *you* have been such a kind and helpful group that my faith in the younger generation has been restored.

Do you like cheese? Will you help me eat the rest of the map?

No, thank you for the thought, but I won't rebuild it. More than half of it is gone anyway. Let's just have a party and eat up the other half. Would you like a wedge of Winnipeg? A sliver of Saskatchewan? A big bite of British Columbia? Perhaps a nibble of Newfoundand?

Please dig in. We'll have ice cream for dessert!

FAMOUS PORTRAIT GALLERY

Famous Dead Canadians speak out — the Plumley Norris version

Tommy Douglas

William Stephenson

Dr. Norman Bethune (centre)

Archie Belaney

Tom Longboat

William Lyon Mackenzie King

Emily Carr

Louis Riel

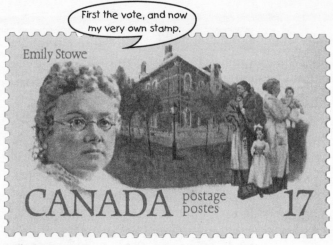

Emily Stowe

Mary Ann Shadd

David Thompson

Thanadelthur

Radisson and Groseilliers

Jean de Brébeuf

Henry Hudson

Illustration Credits

Joanne Stanbridge's *Famous Dead Canadians* is a Silver Birch Honour Book and was shortlisted for the Red Cedar Award, as was her first novel, *The Leftover Kid*. In 1999 the picture book she illustrated, *My Four Lions*, was named an Ontario Library Association Best Bet. Her most recent book, *Who Runs This Country, Anyway?* is a hilarious take on Canadian government for young readers. *Quill & Quire* called it "the best book I've seen on this topic." Joanne lives in Kingston, Ontario.

Bill Dickson's madcap illustrations romp across the pages of *Famous Dead Canadians, First Folks and Vile Voyageurs, Made in Canada, The Scholastic Teacher's Diary* and the cover of *Why Did the Underwear Cross the Road?* Bill lives just a stone's throw away from beautiful Sauble Beach, Ontario, with his wife Eeva and their dog.

Selected Bibliography

Canadian Encyclopedia. On-line. (Includes *Junior Encyclopedia of Canada.*)

Ford, Karen and Janet MacLean and Barry Wansbrough. *Great Canadian Lives: Portraits in Heroism to 1867.* Scarborough, Ont.: Nelson, 1985.

Hancock, Pat. *The Penguin Book of Canadian Biography for Young Readers: Early Canada.* Toronto: Penguin Books, 1999.

Hehner, Barbara. *The Penguin Book of Canadian Biography for Young People,* Vol. 2, 1867–1945. Toronto: Penguin, 2002.

Horizon Canada: *A New Way to Discover the History of Canada.* (10 vols.) Laval, P.Q.: Centre for the Study of Teaching Canada, 1987.

Hudson Bay Company Archives. On-line.

Lloyd, Tanya. *Canadian Girls Who Rocked the World.* Vancouver/Toronto: Whitecap, 2001.

National Library of Canada. *Passageways: True Tales of Adventure for Young Explorers.* On-line.

Peacock, Shane. *Unusual Heroes: Canada's Prime Ministers and Fathers of Confederation.* Toronto: Puffin Canada, 2002.